FROM EXECUTIVE TO ENTREPRENEUR

The A to Z Guide For Female Executives

By Jane W. Lee

Edited by Maja Dezulovic

Copyright © 2016 Jane W. Lee

All rights reserved. No part of this publication may be reproduced, stored in a retrieval system, or transmitted in any form or by any means, electronic, mechanical, photocopying, recording, digital or otherwise, without the prior permission of the publisher.

This book is sold subject to the condition that it shall not by way of trade or otherwise be lent, re-sold, hired out or otherwise circulated without the publisher's prior consent in any form binding or cover other than that in which it is published and without a similar condition including this condition being imposed on the subsequent purchaser.

Table of Contents

PREFACE	1
WHO AM I?	3
SO WHAT'S IN IT FOR YOU?	6
"A" - AGGRESSIVENESS	9
"B" - BRANDING	14
"C" - COMMUNICATION	18
"D" - DIFFERENTIATION	23
"E" - E-COMMERCE	27
"F" - FINANCIAL MANAGEMENT	37
"G" - GLOBALIZATION	41
"H" - HIRING	47
"I" - INSPIRATIONS	52
"J" - JOURNEY	56
"K" - KNOWLEDGE	60
"L" - LEVERAGE	63
"M" - MARKETING	67
"N" - NETWORKING	71

"O" - OPPORTUNITIES	75
"P" - PASSION	79
"Q" - QUALITY	83
"R" - RISK MANAGEMENT	86
"S" - SELF-MOTIVATION	90
"T"- TRUSTWORTHINESS	94
"U" - UPCYCLE	98
"V" - VISION	101
"W" - WORK FROM HOME	105
"X"- X-FACTOR	110
"Y" - YOUNG AT HEART	113
"Z" - ZERO TO ZILLION	117
YOUR JOURNEY	120
ABOUT THE AUTHOR	122

PREFACE

"How did you do it?" they asked me.

"How did you, a married woman with a little boy, choose to leave your senior executive position to start up your own business, and one that involves a lot of 'grunt work' at that?"

Who are "they", you wonder? Well... pretty much everybody. Friends. Family. Professional colleagues. People who knew me by the executive persona I had spent fifteen years carefully crafting.

What was my answer? They were right. After all, I am a Certified Public Accountant (CPA), a profession that isn't exactly crowded with risk-takers. This was one of; if not the biggest risk I've ever taken. The decision to leave the corporate world behind in order to start a business traditionally is.

But why did I do it?

My answer could be summarized by four simple letters: B.Y.O.B.

(Hmmm....I can see how that could be confusing. Now before you jump to conclusions, it's not that "B.Y.O.B." Let me try this again....)

Be Your Own Boss.

(Much better!)

People see these words and it seems, on the surface, to be the American Dream. Freedom. Independence. Setting your own hours. Paving your own way. Being directly responsible for your successes and your failures. For me, it was about the all these things and I wanted to follow my passion. I wanted that freedom and independence. I wanted to be able to see first-hand what happens when people appreciate and respect the work that I do. But perhaps most importantly, I wanted the freedom to spend more time with my family. And maybe this is weird, but there's one thing that didn't drive me as much as the reasons on the aforementioned list: money. Sure I wanted to make money along the way….who doesn't? But I figured that if I did what I truly wanted to do, and I became really good, the money would follow! Also, I wasn't too keen on changing the world with my business. I think I'll leave that to the Mark Zuckerbergs of the world.

But enough about me... I want you to think about YOUR situation! What drives you? What's your passion? Maybe it is money and fame. Or maybe, like me, you want the freedom to make your own way in this world. If you'd like to start your own business, then you will want to read on. This book was put together for you.

WHO AM I?

(OK....so a LITTLE more about me! I mean, you've decided to read this book. You may as well know whose words may or may not be inspiring you to take that unprecedented life-changing leap into business independence.)

How did I become an entrepreneur?

I'd like to say that I was following in my family's footsteps, but that's not true. I could also say that we could afford to have me follow my entrepreneurial dreams to fruition, but that wasn't the case either.

The fact is that entrepreneurship wasn't even on my radar. I was working as a Certified Public Accountant, having studied accounting since I was 15 years old. Once I graduated from college with my accounting degree, I received a pair of lucrative offers from two of the "Big 4" international CPA firms so my path had pretty much been laid out in front of me.

As I climbed my way up the accounting industry ladder, obtaining the necessary qualifications along the way, I actually received another great offer from a commercial firm. At that point, my interest and my focus had shifted from accounting to the internet, specifically e-commerce business. And as luck would have it, I was actually pretty good at it, having received annual promotions en route to reaching the top management levels of the company. For me, this was a pretty valuable lesson: in business, passion without limits can be a lucrative proposition.

It was a journey that had been, at that point, 12 years in the making. My path had been set, and my future was bright. But there was still something missing. And anybody who has taken a similar route to starting a business knows what comes next.

While I had a passion for accounting and e-commerce, my true passion was…. (Drum roll please)… styling with jewelry! I loved the bling and the sparkle of my favorite pieces served as an apt metaphor for the sparkle I needed in my life. For me, being a senior executive, while stable and predictable, was getting kind of boring.

And when my passion met my skill set, I was rolling. In my first quarter alone, not only did I break even, I was also able to obtain exclusive distribution rights from some designer brands in the industry, placing them in some of the premier department stores and outlets in the country. In the first three years my sales multiplied six times.

While the numbers were good (and they were my bread and butter) it was the marketing and networking that helped me cross that chasm into the results I needed to get for this to work. Endorsements for celebrities from around the country and around the world came rolling in. Executives and business leaders were also singing praises for my company. I have even been able to expand my business into the event and wedding planning sector. I was on my way!

In thinking about the accomplishments I've achieved along the way, I often remind myself that this didn't come by accident, nor did it come through my efforts alone. While people have described me as an ambitious, resourceful person hell-bent on getting results, I have, in turn, passed along the kudos and recognition to those who have helped shape my success. That's why I have used my business to reach out to other people like me: career professionals with executive experience. I've been in their shoes and I know the importance of maintaining a balanced lifestyle, which is why I have helped them build businesses similar to mine and why I also helped set up an online executive club called "Achievers' Minds". We share tips and tools about how to grow your business and your life using professional advice from people around the world. Now I want to share this information with you.

SO WHAT'S IN IT FOR YOU?

It's not hyperbole to say that when you start your own business, success really is yours for the taking. All you need to know is where to look and what to look for. A few months ago, somebody asked me, "A lot of business owners are pretty quiet about how they got so successful. Why do you choose to share what makes you different?" I guess it's just in my nature to "pay it forward" and share the guidance that many have given me along my journey. Having already achieved my own desires, and having a system in place to help others on their paths, I figured why not share what I've learned with everybody who needs to it and is searching for it (like those of you reading this book)?

One of the first and most important pieces of advice I could possibly impart is that success does not come overnight and anybody who says otherwise is lying. For me, success didn't even come close to overnight. It wasn't easy, and it still isn't... Few CEO's still cleans the tables every day!

I have made plenty of mistakes along the way, which helped with the learning process. Research. Trial and error. More research. It's all been part of my journey. And it will be a part of yours too. I'd like to say that I wouldn't want you to make the same mistakes that I did, but that's not true, because you need to make mistakes along the way in order to grow and learn from those mistakes.

If you agree, then welcome to my thoughts, my world... my book! Through hard work and determination I did something that neither I, nor anyone else, even dreamed I could do. And you can too! Think of this book as a humble companion you can turn to whenever you get stuck. Maybe the answer to help you resolve your situation lies in these pages. Maybe the answer isn't here, but an encouraging word of wisdom and support, telling you to keep fighting, will be. Either way, I'm here.

And because I know firsthand that the LAST thing entrepreneurs have in abundance is free time, I've kept things pretty short and sweet. In fact, I've broken it down all the way back to when we learned the alphabet, so enjoy the A to Z of entrepreneurship!

Let's get started.

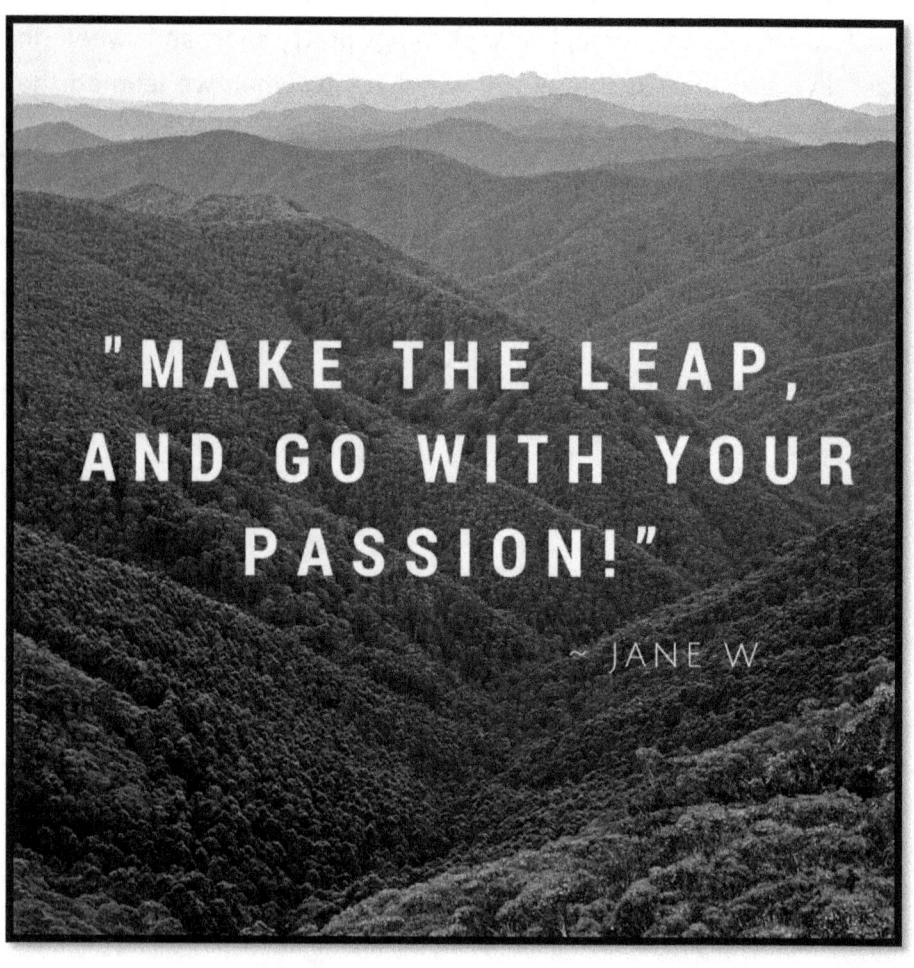

ENTREPRENEURSHIP

A - Z

"A" - AGGRESSIVENESS

It's been said that "nice guys finish last". I'd like to think that I'm a fairly nice person and I've been pretty successful, so I can't say whether or not this is true when it comes to business. I've gotten into many discussions with fellow entrepreneurs about whether or not this is true and the answer has yet to be resolved. One thing I can tell you is that passive people are very unlikely to succeed in business, and even basic assertiveness may not be enough to get your business over the hump.

The importance of being aggressive was one of the first major lessons I learned in starting my own business. Coming into entrepreneurship from my background in accounting, I had come from a world where everything was set and self-contained. Every day I knew what my objectives would be when I got to the office and I knew what I needed to do to achieve them. I knew that I had a budget and I knew that, given that budget, I had to control the spending within the budget. I also understood that I had to get the most "bang" for the buck in terms of maximizing the value and revenue that resulted from what I had spent. And every month I knew I could count on receiving a nice paycheck for my efforts. It was stable. It was comfortable.

Entrepreneurship, on the other hand, provided a lot of elements I was unaccustomed to. Where would my next dollar come from? What lengths would I have to go to make the next sale? These questions, and my approach to answering them, meant the difference between whether or not my family would eat, my people would get paid, and whether my business would even survive. So when it came to what approach to take, I knew instantly that aggressiveness was the way to go. That meant calling on prospects two or three times a day to try to move the sales process along. That meant pushing my staff and contractors out of their comfort zones, thus making my relationships with them uncomfortable, in order to accomplish the goals I needed them to reach. That meant reviewing my expense numbers (to the penny) so I knew where we were spending our money. It didn't matter to me. I knew where I needed to be and I was hell-bent on getting there whatever the figurative, and sometimes literal, cost. Given the type of person I was in the corporate world this transition wasn't an easy one. Thankfully, the change didn't have to be a 100% makeover in my case and it shouldn't be in your case either.

You also have to develop an internal monitor to indicate when you should turn aggressiveness "ON" or "OFF". An example of when the switch should be set to "OFF" is when you are selling. For the most part, you don't need to hard sell your potential customers on your product or service in order to get the results you want. In fact, in my experience, the less hard selling you do, the better off you're going to be. We live in the Information Age. If you're on the fence about a major purchasing decision, how often do you Google the purchase in question? What do you find? Information about the product or service on the company's website. Videos showcasing the product or service's strengths and weaknesses, presented either by the company or by a third party on YouTube. Reviews and data about the product or service on an independent, third party website such as Consumer Reports, Angie's List or Yelp. You are armed to the teeth with the exact information you need to make that decision. What more can a sales pitch presented by somebody who stands to benefit if, and only if, you say "yes" add to that mix of information? The answer: not much.

One way to mitigate the need to be aggressive in your sales approach is to focus on providing a product or service that sells itself and rely primarily on the honesty and transparency that is inherent with what is simply a good product. You'll build credibility in no time.

For me, building that credibility was one of the most important steps I had to take in order to succeed, especially since I was dealing with jewelry, an industry that is plagued with a lack of credibility due to the glut of knockoffs that infiltrate the marketplace. I owned the distribution rights to a brand that had been one of the most successful sellers in England, no small feat considering that over there they had only focused on personal sales or, at most, reaching out to boutiques to sell the brand. But I had done my homework thanks to my accredited jewelry professional study from the Gemological Institute of America (GIA). I knew that my brand had a lot of esteem and even just by looking at the pieces, one could see their beauty and authenticity. So for the Hong Kong distribution channel I figured the best approach would be to "go big" with my sales, calling on buyers of high-end department stores to gauge interest. The conversations were as simple as could be. I showed them the design of the jewelry and described the features and benefits of the product. That was it. The product spoke for itself and my approach was basic and credible. No hard sell necessary!

Aggressiveness can be well-illustrated by the story of two salesmen who went to sell shoes in a foreign country where nobody wore shoes. The first salesman only managed to sell one pair of shoes, then packed his bags and left. He thought it was too difficult to try and sell shoes to people who didn't wear them in the first place. In contrast, the second salesman realized that there was a huge opportunity in this untapped market – if nobody wore shoes, he could sell a pair to every citizen. The second salesman was aggressive in his approach and he took the opportunity presented to him. If you want to be a successful entrepreneur, you need to do the same.

Simply put, sales is the most important element of any business no matter how big or small. Without a sale nothing happens and aggressiveness is the key element when it comes to finding the sales opportunities you need to explore to make your business succeed.

But just as aggressiveness is what drives you to knock on that next door for the opportunity to make the sale, be sure to check that aggressiveness at the door when it opens and let honesty and transparency be your guide when it comes to the sale itself. Roll up your sleeves, take the risk and earn the potential reward.

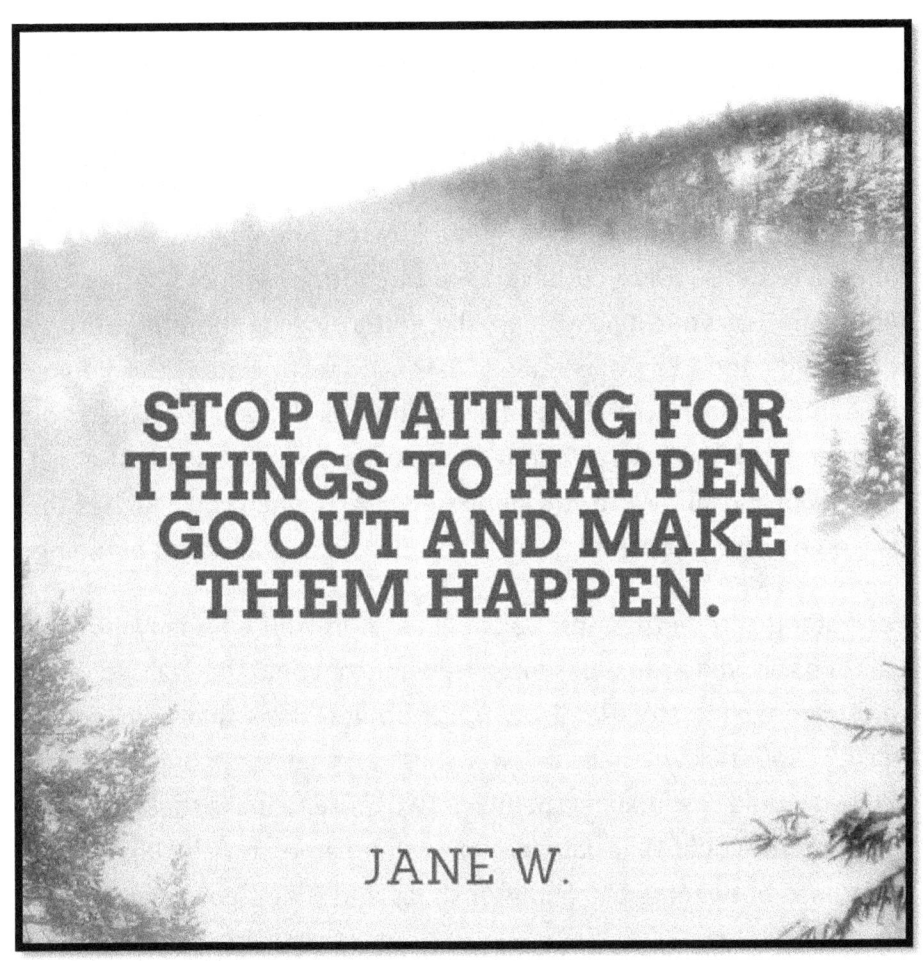

"B" - BRANDING

You know what your company is. You know the product and/or service your company provides. You also know the primary strengths and weaknesses of your product and/or service relative to your competition. But what about your employees? Your industry? Your customers? The marketplace at large? How do they know what your company is? The answer can be summed up in one word: BRANDING.

Our lives are defined, if not dominated by the branding we encounter on a daily basis. Did you have a Venti cup of Starbucks coffee this morning? For your lunch break, did you swing by the drive-thru at McDonald's for a Big Mac Value Meal? And what kind of car did you drive into drive-thru? How many billboards did you see when you drove to work? What cell phone did you use to call your client about the new proposal? Were you inundated by ads when you watched the ballgame on TV last night? You get the picture. It's all about branding.

Your brand can be the most valuable asset in your company. Take a pair of basic white running shoes. How much would that pair go for at the nearest shoe store? How much do you think that pair cost to make? Now throw a pair of "swooshes" on that same pair of shoes. While it would cost maybe a penny or two more to make that pair, how much more would that pair sell for in that same store? What is the difference between a blank pair of shoes and Nike's newest product? Branding.

Branding doesn't just lie in the label on a piece of clothing or a corporate logo. You can brand your company simply by establishing a unique culture that helps your employees become as productive as possible in order to deliver your product or service as effectively as possible. And your employees become extensions of that brand and represent your company much like a pair of shoes with swooshes on them represents a pair of Nike shoes.

A startup can be compared to a baby, and the process of establishing a brand for the company is similar to the process of naming a child. You're creating the identity that your company will become known as. How do you want your company, your "baby", to be perceived in the marketplace? Your branding strategy will determine that answer, both in the present and for years to come.

When it was time to name and brand my company I knew it would be one of the most significant decisions I would have to make. I also knew it had to be right. It had to be an extension of me. So I chose "Fiesta". Why? Well, for one, I wanted to exude a vibe of happiness. What better way than to think of my brand as one big party? The name has personal significance as well. "Fiesta" is the name of one of my son's favorite cartoons. So the name also serves as a reminder of the people who matter most in my life and motivates me to work as hard as I possibly can to provide them with the best life possible.

Successful brands:

If you want to see how good branding works, look at successful global brands. What do you think of when you see the Coca-Cola brand? The drink quenches your thirst and the brand has become synonymous with refreshment. This message has been echoed throughout the company's marketing campaign for years.

What comes to mind when you think of McDonald's? You may be busy and need to get a quick meal so you'll think of driving through to

McDonald's. That's exactly what the brand represents – fast food! You don't want to go to a McDonald's and have to wait half an hour for your meal. That's not what you were promised.

Both these brands have taken a lot of heat lately regarding their contribution to a declining rate of health due to poor nutrition. But, let's try to remember that health is not what their branding represents. They deliver what we have come to expect. It is our responsibility to accept or reject the consequences of our consumption choices.

Remember that a company's brand is often an extension of the culture and the people that set up that brand. So make it count, and make it consistent with the strategy and objectives that drive your company. The truer you are to your brand, the more everybody involved with its growth can buy in, the harder they'll work, the more effective the company will be and the more profits you'll enjoy sooner rather than later. Who knows? Your brand could be the next Nike, Walmart or Starbucks (...or even bigger!)

"C" - COMMUNICATION

Here's a challenge for you: Go one day without engaging in communication with anybody. No phone calls. No emails. No texts. No face-to-face conversations. It's impossible, right? (And if it is possible, you're likely living on a deserted island.) I'd be willing to bet that in this day and age it would be pretty tough to go through one waking hour without communication with the outside world. For an entrepreneur like myself, often I can't go a minute without communicating with somebody. That's right! 60 seconds! Effective communication is therefore an essential component of an entrepreneur's skill set. It has to be. If you're like I was before I made "the leap", you're probably thinking to yourself: "Heck, I've been working at my current profession for (x) years. I know how to communicate. No problem!"

Not so fast…

In my case, I was pretty blunt back in the day. I would not hesitate to say exactly what was on my mind whether or not it was, objectively, the right call. Like most of my colleagues in the corporate world, I was playing defense. Company politics often dictated that I had to. I worked hard my entire career to earn my spot, and it was quite the lucrative spot at my "peak". I had gotten what I had wanted. Now I had to keep that spot and protect it from all corners.

Then I made the leap.

I quickly, if not immediately, realized that the communication style that got me through my life as an accountant would not fly as an entrepreneur. I couldn't be as blunt as I had been. There was too much to lose by potentially saying the wrong thing at the wrong time to the wrong person and costing my company a big opportunity. On top of that I had to learn the value of communication to my business. Every word mattered. Every intonation and inflection in my voice was relevant. Every hesitation could have been a deal breaker. Every word I printed had to reflect my true thoughts and ideas. Multiply this by every communication I had with my partners, clients, vendors, customers, prospects, and all the way down to the man or woman on the street. That's how valuable and significant good communication can be.

Here's something that shocked me when I started my entrepreneurial journey: Communication is a two-way street. I could sit here and tell you about how good my jewelry is. Features. Benefits. The whole nine yards. And at the end of that monologue, where mine was the only voice in the picture, you could tell me that you had no interest whatsoever. Why? Because it's not what you wanted. And if I had made listening to you a priority and had afforded you the opportunity to tell me what you wanted right off the bat then I would have known that. In a broader sense, I would have understood your needs and what problems my product or service could solve. That way, I would have been able to focus my pitch on your issues and requirements.

The technology that permeates the world in which we live has transformed how we communicate by leaps and bounds. When I first started my professional career, and I suspect this may hold true for you too, most professional communication was executed via phone and face-to-face interaction and for the adventurous among us – the facsimile. Email was just coming into play, which begat other online forms of communication as well as text/SMS messaging among the myriad of options we have today.

If you're an entrepreneur who has international clientele, as I do for both my jewelry and my wedding businesses, the choices you have for communication are godsends in terms of efficiency and cost-effectiveness. If, for example, I was working with a wedding couple who wanted to get married in Hong Kong but live overseas, I have the option to not only communicate via email (one of the few ways that doesn't cost much and is not impeded by differences in time zones) but also through phone, Skype or other means. This ensures that we're all on the same page and that nothing gets lost in literal or cultural translation, which would be the last thing that anybody planning a wedding would want to happen.

Another important lesson for me to learn along the way, and this goes along with the idea that communication is a two-way street, was how others prefer to communicate. Case in point: For my jewelry business, I remember having to call on a critical vendor for a rather urgent matter pertaining to my Hong Kong distribution center. Getting no answer, I left a message then called back the next day to follow up. Still nothing. This went on for days. Furious at what I had perceived to be rude, unprofessional behavior, I sent a terse email about the matter. Five minutes later, I found a confused, defensive reply email in my inbox. When I had explained that I had tried to call, the other party had indicated that they "pretty much never take calls", adding that email was a much more effective way for that person to communicate. I was aghast. How was this even possible? Upon further review, I took a step back and realized that how this person chose to communicate with others wasn't up to me. From that point on we had a very effective, fruitful email-only working relationship. And from that I learned to cover all of my bases from Day One. If I need to reach someone, first I call. Then leave a voicemail. Then I email about the call. Then I call about the email about the call. You see the pattern. If after a few days of this pattern, there's still silence on the other end then I guess, as the saying goes, they're just not that into me.

However you choose to communicate, you must realize that, just as I indicated that you are your brand, so is your communication. How you communicate is reflective of how you want others to view you. I'll never forget a workshop I attended where the presenter beat it into our brains that "whatever you do, try to let the people around you feel happy too." I'm an upbeat person and as a result I try to keep my communication as upbeat as possible even if the message involved is inherently negative. This approach has generally served me well even in the face of the occasional obscenity-laden (and in the age of email, ALL CAPS) communication strategy employed by the other party in the discourse.

So, learn to not judge other people but instead, to appreciate the good things around. You will gain respect in return.

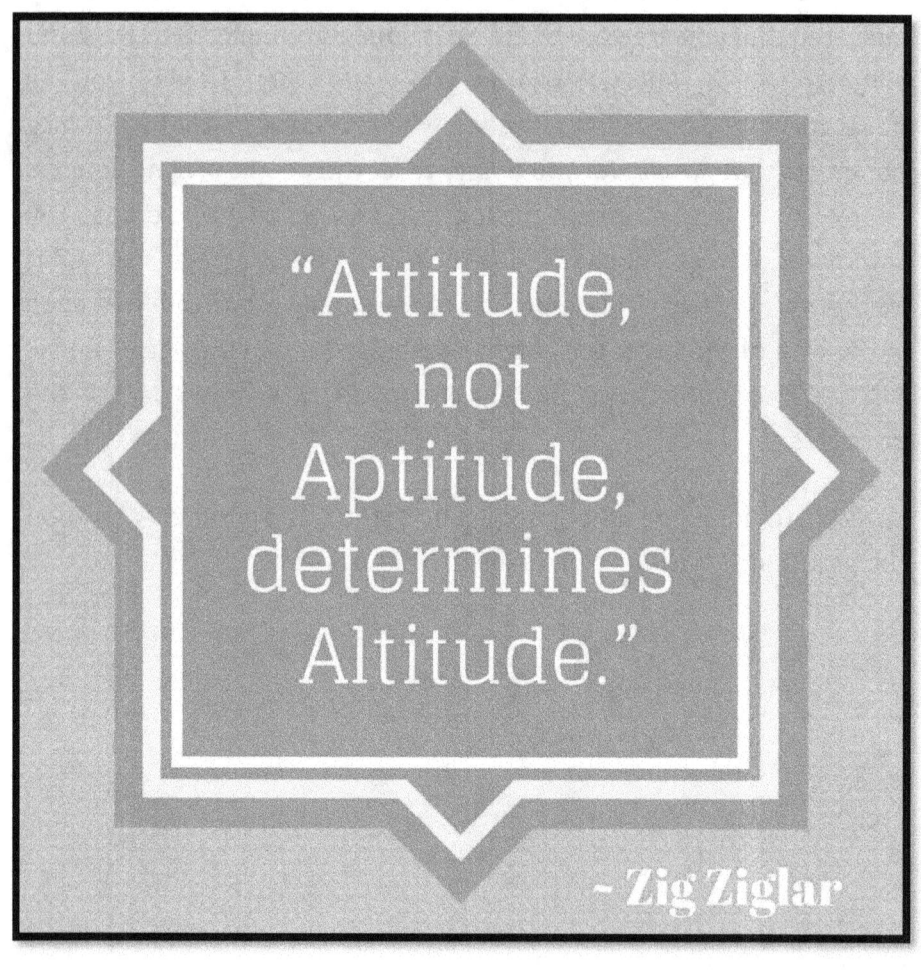

"D" - DIFFERENTIATION

Think back to your childhood. One of the first lessons imparted to you by teachers and the world at large was probably the idea that we're all different and that it's good to be different. "No two snowflakes are the same" we were taught. Fast forward to your experience as a nascent entrepreneur and you'll find that the snowflake analogy is especially apt for business as well. No two businesses are alike. Not even close. From leadership to operational philosophy to your deliverable product or service, there are an abundance of differences between your company and others in your chosen industry. You know this, but the trick is to get your target market to know this and that means putting your competitive advantages front and center in everything you do. Maybe even get a tattoo depicting these competitive advantages!

In startup mode, many entrepreneurs plan as if their companies exist in a vacuum, devoid of competition. They plan to develop an idea, manufacture and market that idea and finally, how to deliver upon that idea to the marketplace at large. Then they'll watch the profits roll in. Simple, right? But what happens when you find out that there's another company (if not five, ten, or even more) that are doing the exact same thing that you do? And worse, they're doing it better, faster, and cheaper. Surely, you didn't plan for this, right? You couldn't have!

Sadly, yes, you could have, and you should have. Researching the potential competition you'll face when you "go live" with your company is one of the most essential components you'll need to address during the planning stages. Knowing their competitive advantages and disadvantages will put you in a better position to establish yours, and to communicate yours to the marketplace. Unfortunately this isn't just information you can tack onto the bulletin board on Day One and forget about it. In any industry the competitive advantages and disadvantages held by all of the industry's companies can change on an annual, quarterly, monthly, or even weekly basis. You need to be kept abreast of these changes on a daily basis in order to be successful.

How you differentiate your product or service from your competition can be the jumping off point for a number of different elements of your business strategy, from how you price your deliverable (cheaper or higher end) to how you advertise it (Wall Street Journal or your local Pennysaver) to where you distribute it (Macy's or Walmart). The decisions you make when it comes to differentiation, and your ability to execute on these decisions, could be a significant source of value creation for your company.

Differentiation has always been a priority in my companies and the results reflect how good a decision that has been. My wedding planning business is an example. When you evaluate a standard wedding planning package, you usually factor in a pretty stable price structure that encompasses the basic necessities of a traditional wedding (gown, photography and videography service, makeup and hair, venue, etc.). You're paying for the right to "set it and forget it" by putting the legwork in the hands of my or another wedding planning company. I knew right away that I had to be different, based on the research I did on my competition. So I chose to vary the price I charge for my service, as opposed to having a standard price in place. I would work with the couple to understand their specific needs and budget that they had to work with. Taking that budget into consideration, I was able to match them with the exact vendors and suppliers to fit their needs; and not only on price, but also on quality, as I had professional, quality working relationships with each of them. I leveraged my personal relationships with my vendors to negotiate a price that would ultimately save, on average, 15-20% off their original budget. (And as anybody who has ever planned a wedding knows, staying under budget, by any percentage, let alone 15-20%, is almost as much cause for celebration as the wedding itself!) I was able to differentiate myself on a number of different factors, all related directly to each other. I am able to differentiate on my experience, and it was through that experience that I was able to work with a number of vendors over the years which, in turn, enabled me to differentiate on the choices I could offer to my clients. I also leveraged my longstanding relationships with these vendors to lower prices for their services, a saving I was able to pass along to the customer, enabling me to differentiate on price as well. All in all, I was able to provide my clients with an option based on experience and I was able to grant them access to a number of different vending options at a rate far less than what they were expecting to pay. I can't devise a better recipe for success than that!

Now it's time for you to find your recipe for success. What do you do differently compared to your competition? And how can you capitalize on this? The answers are entirely in your hands…..all you need to do is do the work!

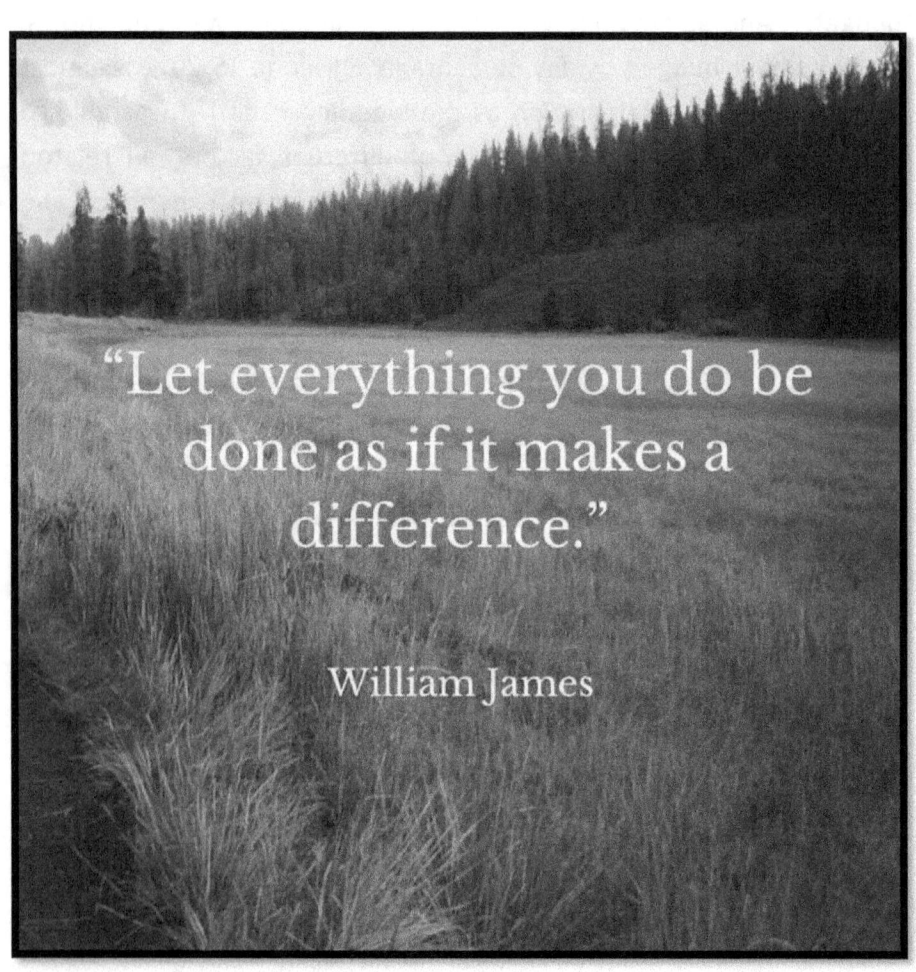

"E" - E-COMMERCE

Pop quiz time!

I just want you to see how on the ball you are when it comes to e-commerce.

What is the significance of the following dates: July 5th, 1994 and September 3rd, 1995?

Give yourself a couple of minutes to answer (without Google), then read on.

Those dates, 14 months apart in time, signify the dawn of the "twin towers" of e-commerce, Amazon and Ebay, respectively. As the "world wide web" was emerging as a potential force in our society, Jeff Bezos (Amazon) and Pierre Omidyar (Ebay) had visions of how this revolutionary technology could be used to create virtual stores, encompassing everything from providing the virtual catalog to managing the payment and compensation structure, to establishing a distribution system, and to policing the process to ensure that both vendor and customer are satisfied. Though nobody knew it at the time, those two business models were the basis and impetus for millions of online-based businesses, mine included, that have come down the pike since. Billions of dollars have changed hands online in the almost twenty years since these two businesses opened their virtual doors. Not bad for a few of lines of code!

E-commerce has been an extreme game changer when it comes to the success of a business. A retail-based business is no longer bound by the limitations of a "brick and mortar" storefront in terms of location, hours of operation, manpower, and inventory. E-commerce has levelled the playing field in a big way, enabling a "single shingle" establishment to have the same online pull as a "big box" store, such as Walmart, Best Buy, or Home Depot. Companies have the power to reach customers all over the world at any time of day (and achieving the ideal of "making money while you sleep").

It's all well and good in the big picture, but you may be thinking: "What's in it for me?" How can you start your own e-commerce business?

Whether you are looking to expand the reach of your brick and mortar store or simply starting anew from Jump Street, there really is no bad time to start an e-commerce business. The opportunities are practically limitless.

But where do you start?

1. WEBSITE

Much like a physical establishment would have required a location back in the day, your first step in starting a business is establishing the virtual storefront known as your website. In the age where search engine optimization (SEO) is king, what will you do to ensure that visitors (Googlers) find your store when they're looking for the product in which you specialize? "But Jane," you may be thinking right now, "I don't know HTML code from a bar code! How in the world could I ever build a website?" Just as you may not be comfortable building your own storefront brick-by-brick, you may not be comfortable building your own website, which is totally fine. Knowing your own limitations is essential for an entrepreneur so it's important to know what you don't know. All you need to know is a "rough draft" for what you want your website to be, then find the right web developer to help get you started, and the right program to help you manage the site on your own.

One of the first decisions you need to make is what to call your website. Is it going to be as direct as www.(your name here).com? Is it going to be a play on a popular catch phrase or something reflecting the town in which you operate? Is it going to be a "dot com", "dot biz" or some other domain name? Most importantly, are those options even available for you to use?

Once you decide on a name and verify its availability, the next step is to purchase the domain name, so it is yours. Purchasing this website address would be akin to paying rent on the land on which your brick-and-mortar store operates, but even more amazingly, you're doing this for just a few bucks per year! From there, you can work with your developer on just how you want your site to look and the functionality you want on the site, from both yours and the user's perspective. A common strategy along these lines is to have yourself or your developer host the site directly and to implement turnkey software exclusive to the web building process, such as Squarespace or WordPress. These programs are quite easy for even a "tech-unsavvy" user to be able to control the majority of the content on the site and update it as needed.

2. A PERSONAL EMAIL

In my section on branding, I stressed the importance of your brand as a reflection of yourself. The same idea holds true for your email address as a reflection of how you want your company to be perceived.

Say you're at a networking event, one in which you encounter a number of professionals from different types of businesses, each of whom could be a potential vendor to help you grow and develop. And as it so happens, you meet two attorneys at separate points in the event, but both of whom are named Joe Smith (Esquire). You have pleasant conversations with both Joes, and in the process of networking, they hand you their business cards. When you get back to the office, you revisit their cards. Joe Smith #1 has an email address of "joe@josephsmithesq.com", while Joe Smith #2 has an email address of "joesmithesq@hotmail.com". Presuming all other things to be equal (same name, same profession, same level of experience, same length and quality of conversation at the event), which Joe Smith would you be more inclined to contact the next day? For me, it's a no-brainer. If I encounter a colleague with a professional email account in the same email domain (Hotmail, Yahoo, Gmail, etc.) that one of my kids can use for theirs, it gives me the impression that the person doesn't have the commitment to invest the nominal fee or effort into a personalized email account (and a chance to brand the company in the process).

Another pet peeve for me, as a frequent emailer of businesses in hopes of reaching somebody specific to communicate on a certain topic, is to have to send something to an impersonal, catch-all "info@xyz.com" address. When I encounter one of those, that's pretty much a red flag warning me that there's a good chance this message will never be read, let alone replied to. For my companies, I pride myself on using the real names as well as targeted group email addresses (for example: "sales@xyz.com", "pr@xyz.com", "manufcaturing@xyz.com") that automatically get forwarded to everyone in that department, increasing the likelihood that somebody will get back to the emailer sooner rather than later.

In this day and age, email is on par with, if not superseded completely, telephone as the foremost way to communicate with one another on the marketplace. Do your part to look professional and make it easy for people to communicate with you.

3. PAYPAL SERVICE/CREDIT CARD ACCEPTANCE

Imagine walking into a store to buy a gallon of milk, and when you go to pay for it, the clerk tells you that they do not accept the form of payment you are attempting to use. Would you go to another store? Would you try to find another way to pay for the milk? Who's right in this case? Technically, both the store and the customer are right. The store has the right to accept whatever forms of payment it wants to, no matter how feasible or unfeasible they may be, and the customer has the right to adhere to these restrictions or to take their business elsewhere.

This analogy is not limited to brick-and-mortar stores as it also extends to e-commerce as well. Since you can't accept cash to complete an online deal (it would also be a nightmare if two different currencies were involved) and it would be foolish to accept a check, that leaves credit and/or debit cards as the way to pay. In modern times, even card purchases are risky with the incidence of high-profile hacking and credit card/identity fraud. Enter Paypal, the online payment system, now owned and operated as part of the Ebay umbrella. Paypal changed the game in terms of how payments are universally exchanged across the world, spanning a myriad of currencies. Despite many online payment competitors that have cropped up since Paypal established in 1998, none have been the model of efficiency that Paypal has which is why it remains the go-to option for the majority of all Ebay and many other e-commerce transactions.

4. EMAIL CAMPAIGN SYSTEM

So you just made a sale for your business! Or you just made a bevy of potentially valuable connections at a trade show. Time to file them away, forgetting to acknowledge those people again, right? Wrong! Every contact you make is important. Each person with whom you interact is a contact for the life of your business and potentially a repeat customer. But how do you maintain that customer interaction, especially since you can't guarantee that they will return to you on their own volition? The primary way to do this would be through a systematic, consistent email distribution campaign. Reaching out to your customer base on a quarterly, monthly, weekly, or even daily basis can inform your contacts about what new products or services you are rolling out, and engage them to interact with you to best express the ideas they have about your company.

Creating compelling, actionable, frequent email communication may come across as a daunting task, but much like web design and development, there are numerous online platforms, including MailerMailer, Mailchimp and Aweber, that can transform even the most ardent Luddite into an email marketing master. To establish an effective campaign that actually engages your target base, there are two significant obstacles you must overcome. First, you must "rise above the noise" with your message. To give you an idea of how to do this, look no further than your own inbox. If you're like me, you're an information junkie who wants to be as informed as possible on the latest trends impacting your industry, your competition, your colleagues, and your vendors.

For starters, you can use the email to not only promote your message, but also give value to the person receiving it. Maybe it's literal value in the form of a percentage discount off a product or service, or perhaps it's content value in the form of industry commentaries or insight pieces that give the recipient the information he or she needs to get better with the business. Once you establish that your email is worth the recipient's time to open, you've earned a significant leg up on the competition, in this case the myriad of other emails in a recipient's inbox. Yours is the one that gets the magical "click". The second obstacle to overcome is more serious, especially from a legal point of view. The recently enacted CAN-SPAM Act sets the guidelines for businesses that use email to get the word out about their product or service. Businesses must now be mindful of not only of what they're sending, but also how often and most importantly, whether or not the target recipient wants to receive their message. Ensuring that your recipient can opt in to receive your message is a must when establishing an email campaign. This entails that, in no uncertain terms, you must let any target recipient know in advance that you intend to include his or her email address in your mailing list and if that person objects, you must remove them from your recipient list immediately.

5. SOCIAL MEDIA

When Mark Zuckerbug came up with the idea for Facebook a decade ago, it was intended to be an interactive way for Harvard University students to get to know each other better. Little did he know how big his site would become, nor did he know that his site would revolutionize how individuals interact with each other and how businesses interact with their target audience. In this age of viral online content, where one "like" can turn into 10, then 100 likes in an instant, business owners are rapidly realizing the value of establishing a presence on social media sites such as Facebook, LinkedIn, Twitter, Google Plus, Pinterest, and others.

The most beautiful part of social media can be summed up in two words: free advertising! For a business owner, it's as simple as looking at the numbers. While it would be a nice thing to be able to build your database organically and through word of mouth, you can't ignore what's going on in a place like Facebook where there are over a billion users on a monthly basis, most of whom are ready, willing, and able to share what they like with their friends and colleagues multiple times per day. The eyeballs alone are worth the presence.

With so many sites out there, with so many potential new customers who need to be reached in so many different ways, where do you begin? A good, cost-effective strategy may be to find a social media consultant, or for the more budget-conscious, a social media intern.

Despite the fact that it doesn't cost a dime to have a presence on the most popular social media sites, it wouldn't hurt to set aside a social media budget. You can use this to hire the aforementioned freelance consultant, or you could use it to purchase a social media management software package through a site like Hootsuite. These sites are designed to automatically post the content you want to post when you want to post it to as many different sites as you need – a time-saving godsend, considering the alternative is to hop on these different sites and post the content yourself. And if you also have a special event or new product or service you want to promote, you can use some of the budget to promote this on sites like Facebook through paid promotional posts.

"F" - FINANCIAL MANAGEMENT

"How's your cash?" I remember having a conversation with a successful serial entrepreneur, and he told me that those three words were the first words he asked as soon as he walked into the office. Every morning. Without fail. No "Hi." No "How are you?" He always asks: "How's your cash?" If you are not an entrepreneur and you just read that, you might not understand at first, but as an entrepreneur you will learn that cash-flow is literally the lifeblood of a business. It's what keeps your people paid, your goods manufactured, your marketing and advertising humming and your overall infrastructure in place. Without it, none of these things can happen.

You could even say it's the lifeblood of this book. Consider the other chapters, and how, when you break them down to their essence, they are glorified explanations of ways to either attain or save more cash.

Yes, I'm biased. Of course somebody with a certified accounting background would emphasize the importance of cash-flow! But that's not where my bias lies. It lies in wanting to make money and to be successful. Does this mean that you too, need to be a CPA to run a successful business? No. (CPA's that have gone under are sadly nodding their heads in agreement right now.) But it does mean that you need to make money management a top priority that should be addressed daily in your business. You need to know every revenue source and every cost to the penny, for that is the only way that you'll know the baseline from which you can devise your strategy to improve on both of these. And while simply knowing these is important, tracking them is what matters. On a monthly basis, you should establish a monthly P & L (profit and loss) statement so that you know exactly where your money is going, so that you can address the weak spots and reinforce the strong points. Many entrepreneurs consider this a necessary evil, recognizing the importance of keeping track of the finances, but groaning every time they have to sit down and crunch the numbers. In their heads, they can be spending that time doing anything else in order to move the company forward. For me, it's the exact opposite. I love this stuff. And not just because of my CPA background. More often than not, seeing where the numbers fall in my business gives me a second wind to boost sales and cut costs. It renews my mental energy and reinvigorates my focus.

If you're like me and want that rush off to do this yourself, then getting the proper software is a must. It starts with a basic spreadsheet, which you can access using workplace software suites that are available for Windows (Excel) or Mac (Numbers), or even online through Google or other online office platforms. But while having spreadsheets is good for seeing the numbers as they exist, and playing around with them to suit your needs, you need to purchase a financial management software program that puts these numbers in context, and helps make sense of exactly what is happening with your company's finances. Go to any office or computer store and you'll see dozens of choices when it comes to financial management software. For my businesses, I prefer to go with the tried and true Quickbooks program. Quickbooks is simple to use and geared exactly to small businesses like mine, giving the functionality that I need without clogging me with information and metrics that I don't need. (And if I ever do scale up to that level, I can simply upgrade to a higher level of Quickbooks.)

For the entrepreneurs for whom this is a hassle, accounting, bookkeeping and general financial management are typically the first and easiest functions that a business can outsource to a licensed professional, somebody like my pre-entrepreneurial self. Finding the right financial manager at a price that won't break your budget can be a lifesaver for a busy entrepreneur who just wants to go, go, go all the time.

It's been said that money "is the root of all evil", but in business it's the root of all you do. Treating it with the respect and reverence that it deserves should be a top-level priority as you move forward with your business.

> **UNLESS YOU CONTROL YOUR MONEY, MAKING MORE WON'T HELP. YOU'LL JUST HAVE BIGGER PAYMENTS.**
>
> Anonymous

"G" - GLOBALIZATION

"Think Globally, Act Locally."

While these four words have been the mantra for the environmental movement for decades, the "think globally" actually has a lot of merit in the business world as well. It should be in an entrepreneur's second nature to go big, whatever the venture or enterprise may be. It's only natural that, if you feel passionate about something – be it business or otherwise, you'd want to be as thorough as you can to see it through.

For me, thinking globally was a priority from Day One. It definitely helped that I started my jewelry business in Hong Kong, the same place in which I was born and raised. As I was growing up, global enterprise had already been a significant part of the commercial culture of the region, so you really couldn't help but want to make your own business one that spanned the globe. Besides the inherent inspiration from a cultural standpoint, there were also some very real strategic and tactical considerations involved in my decision to go global. For one, establishing our business on a global level would do wonders for our brand, especially seeing as much of our local competition still had a boutique mentality that would be better suited for the smaller markets and shops owned and operated by people who don't have the vision to think beyond their current situation. Plus, going global would open up a seemingly infinite array of opportunities to reach not only new customers who would be intrigued by what I had to offer, but also new vendors, thus giving me yet another edge over rivals that wouldn't know where to turn in order to acquire new merchandise.

While "going global" may sound daunting at first, in practice, it's actually even more daunting than it sounds. I learned that the hard way. It started with the significant investment of time, money and resources it requires to make the leap into a global market. For many looking to make the move, those factors can be immediate deal-breakers. That doesn't begin to include factors such as differences in culture between the international markets, which could be significant as they could be extremely costly in terms of the time it takes for those differences to be ironed out, be it at the management level between the two companies or the marketing level. (Ask yourself: Does an advertising message that works in one country effectively translate to another?)

Just like you would do when you start a business in your own country, for a local market, the key to doing effective international business is to do your homework. Even boning up on such minutiae as export custom and duty regulations could go a long way to saving you significant headaches as you encounter critical importing and exporting decisions.

Some other areas that are worth considering when it comes to preparing your company to go global:

- Assemble your local troops for each market you enter. Build a network of local people who have earned your trust and who can be your eyes and ears as you explore new markets. Bring them aboard your team as agents or sales representatives and let them prove their worth from there, or do some advance research to find a business partner or two in that market who would be willing to invest in what you're doing.

- Take the time to know the languages and cultures, both business and societal, of each market you will be entering. Make sure the aforementioned "boots on the ground" in these markets know their way around them. Do they know how to communicate the right way? Can they effectively market and sell what you are doing to the target customer base in that market? This is critical to the effectiveness of your foray into these countries.

- I can't stress enough the importance of knowing the costs of doing international business in terms of export custom/duties, taxes, etc. This knowledge must be as comprehensive as possible, as certain imports entering certain markets can have a significant set of export fees attached. (Case in point: for my jewelry to enter the Chinese market, the custom import duties in place for this "privilege" are over 20%).

- Know the political and economic situations/history/structure of the companies that you want to enter. How stable is the market? Is it an emerging market? Is there political unrest, or threat of upheaval in the works? How stable is the currency? Is there a threat of economic collapse? What is the backup plan? Knowing these factors in advance could mitigate the risk you potentially face as you enter a potentially explosive situation.

- Know the local licensing regulations for the markets you will be entering. What license(s) do you need to sell your product or service? How far down the governmental chain do these licenses reach? (Are you going country by country? State by state? Borough by borough?) Where do you go to obtain these? What rights are granted under these licenses (and what isn't allowed)? What is the process to obtain these licenses and certifications?

- Take advantage of the resources in your country to get a leg up on what you need to do to succeed outside of your home nation. Find a trade association for your business, as these organizations are in place to support your growth and development. Once you're in with these groups, they'd be happy to give you all of the information, contacts and any administrative support you may need for a successful entry into an international market. That's why they're there. And because they ultimately win when you win, most of the support they are able to provide to you comes at a small, if any cost. (For me, the Hong Kong Trade Development Council was a godsend. When I reached out to them, they were able to provide me with a top-shelf database that I was able to use for many different research projects and most of what they were able to provide was absolutely free!)

- Seek out any potential "test runs" for your international foray by participating in some overseas exhibitions. This gives you an inside look at how customers in these countries think and act when it comes to their purchasing habits. Can the product or service that you provide match up with what they're actually buying? If so, you may be onto a winning formula!

- You may have a friend in government, believe it or not! Something as simple as a Google search may result in your happening upon any number of government funding initiatives for potential subsidies. For my jewelry business, the majority of my overseas exhibitions were subsidized by the Hong Kong government to the tune of 50%. Those numbers can go a long way.

- Prepare for your success in international markets...before, during and after! Work with your local representatives to devise a foolproof guarantee policy that will enable potential buyers to purchase from you with confidence. Granted, the quality of your product or service should speak for itself, right?

If it is, your refund rate should be pretty manageable if you can back up your marketing with the quality of your product.

On the surface, each of these missives seems daunting for even the biggest of businesses, let alone a startup entrepreneur. But speaking as that startup entrepreneur, I can tell you that it's a lot easier for somebody in your position to go global than it is for a behemoth corporation. You're smaller, quicker, and more nimble with your ability to operate and make essential decisions without running them up multiple flagpoles at a glacial place, thanks to big company politics. Perhaps your first step in going global should be to "level the playing field" and set up a website that has the look, the feel, and most importantly, the functionality of a company with vast overseas experience, and let your passion and desire to conquer the world with your business drive you along.

> "Think little goals and expect little achievements. Think big goals and win big success."
>
> — DAVID J. SCHWARTZ

"H" - HIRING

Imagine that you just purchased a machine for your manufacturing plant. Technically, you leased it and the cost of the lease is $5,000/month and that doesn't include additional costs like ongoing maintenance costs as well as costs payable to your government for the right to operate this particular piece of machinery. Now, imagine that you just purchased 10 of these. They all have a different makeup, and all come from different places but you expect them to perform the same task at an optimal level. You would expect there to be a manual for these new devices, right?

Well how come there isn't one for the hiring process? Because that is the exact same thing you are doing, in a sense. There are many different schools of thought when it comes to hiring and for good reason, as each individual hire you make is essentially a significant investment...and a gamble, especially for a startup entrepreneur. Make the right call and you can begin to build a staff that can compete with any company of any size in the industry. Make the wrong decision and it could be a backbreaker, both in terms of the wasted money and time you have invested in an employee that couldn't perform the required tasks.

At the end of the day, business success boils down to the idea of minimizing risk while maximizing return and nowhere is this risk/reward ratio more prominent or important than the hiring. If you're a startup entrepreneur, the first hire or two you make are going to be the most critical. It's pretty much a given that at no other point during the evolution of your company will you be boosting your labor force by 50% at once, which is exactly what will happen when you bring on a second person in your company. So before you make the next hire, ask yourself the following questions:

- Why are you hiring this person? When I was growing my company, I made sure that the first couple of employees I hired were specifically folks whose skill sets complemented my own. While I knew what my strengths were, I also knew what my weaknesses were, and I specifically sought out individuals who could help me by augmenting the skills in which I needed some help. The one thing I did not do, at least early on, was hire a "clone" of myself. I was already devoting all of my energy into the company, so I knew that in the first few months my skill sets were completely covered. When I grew the company to the point where I just couldn't successfully devote all of my energies to running the business and I wished there were two of me, that's when I began looking to hire somebody who was exactly like me (or, close to it, anyway).

- How do you know this is the right person? On the surface, hiring the right person seems like a no-brainer. You have a spot to fill. You bring in a potential hire for an interview. You like that person's resume. You check the references, and they check out. You ask that person some questions, and you like the answers. You hire that person. And both you and your new hire go on to live happily ever after, growing your company to bigger and better things every day... If only it were that simple. And it may very well be that simple for a low-level hire for your company. But for the top level executives, people on whom you need to be able to count on, you need to go a step further. I can't emphasize enough how important an administration of an employee assessment form, such as the Predictive Index (or "PI" for short), is for hiring new people. Tests such as the PI allow you to deep dive into the emotional and psychological makeup of prospective hires to get a feel for how they perceive themselves and how they feel they are perceived by others. As the employer, you need to fill out a psychological profile for the ideal candidate for a particular position you are looking to fill and administer the PI to your prospective hire. The closer the match, the better the chances that the hire will be a good fit for your position.

- What about those references…? So you checked out the resume of your potential hire and you liked what you saw. You called the references listed on the resume (or the ones that were "available upon request") and they had nothing but glowing things to say.

If you answer positively to the above questions, maybe it's a match made in heaven, right? Not so fast…. Go back and double check that resume. Let's say, for example, that the prospective hire listed five previous positions of employment. And let's say that he or she provided three references to contact, for the three longest tenures of employment on that resume. For a savvy employer, this could potentially signify a giant red flag. What about those other two jobs? What happened? Why were they shorter tenures than the other three jobs? The absence of references may indicate a reticence on behalf of the prospective hire to discuss those two jobs, but doesn't that seem like something you'd want to know about, before you bring this person aboard? Again, if it's a low-level hire for your company, you may not be able to afford the time or resources to sweat this every time it comes up. But for a higher-level hire, doing the research to fill in these gaps is a must. Figure out how to get in touch with these companies. Contact the receptionist. Ask about the potential hire. Try to find somebody who worked with him or her (or better yet, supervised that person). Talk to that contact about your potential hire. You'd be much more likely to get the real information, good or bad, about your prospective hire than you would from somebody who is pre-conditioned to offer a series of platitudes.

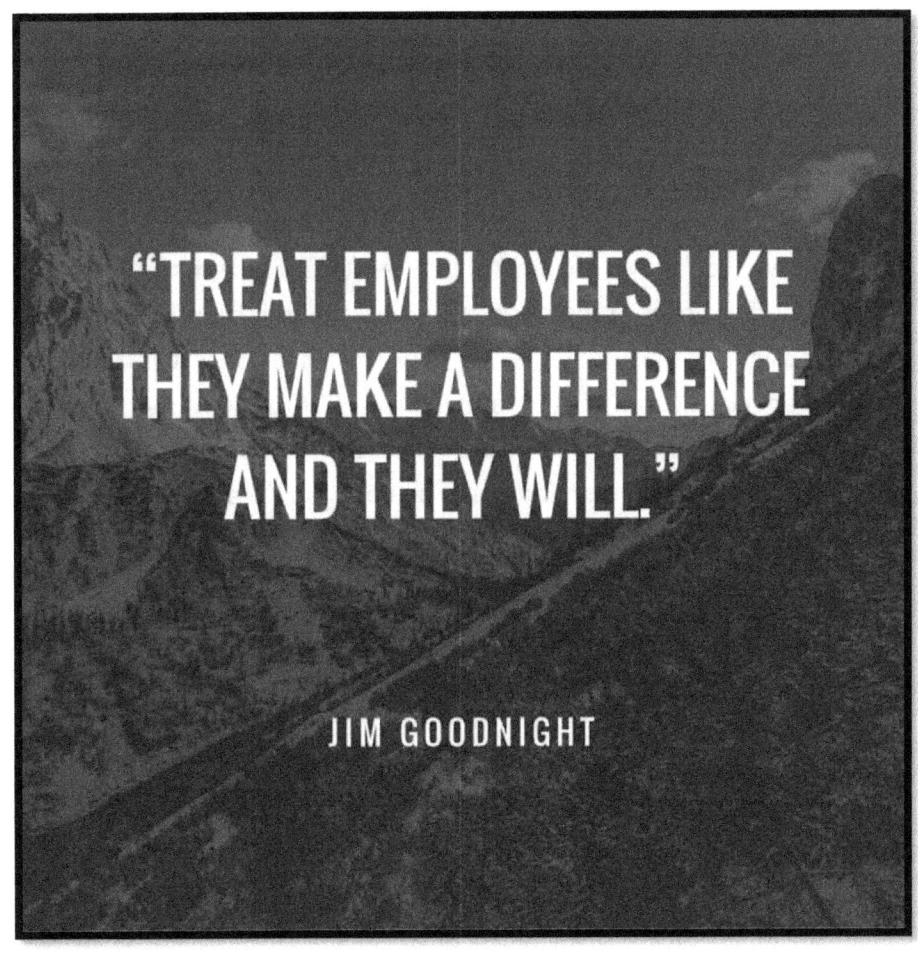

"I" - INSPIRATIONS

Are you a person who always finds opportunities around them? I am and I always love dreaming about how to bring these opportunities to life. Inspirations, ideas, whatever you choose to call them – they are the driving force that gives life to entrepreneurs to pursue their dreams. I think people do have unlimited creativity, it is just a matter of tapping into it. It all goes down to proper planning and strategy so that you also know what to do with this abundance of creativity.

Although we did follow the general marketplace rules for setting a cap on our working hours in the business, meetings with clients in this first period easily ran past that as we gave our best to organize each couple's special event. If you come from a CPA background like me, you will understand why we didn't like to set boundaries on the number of meetings or working hours on each job. Deadline is deadline. We get used to meeting each tax deadline, the Annual General Meeting deadline, etc. And in wedding planning, our deadline is the wedding day, and no matter what has been left unfinished or unchecked, it will be our job to meet the deadline. The show must go on. The couples, their families, and the guests might not see what happens behind the stage (and often you don't want them to), but they will be the ones enjoying their big day without having to worry (we do all the worrying for them).

Tapping into our creativity is one of the essential elements of brainstorming ideas with my colleague. After having spent the first two years getting into the nitty-gritty side of things in terms of running the business, and for me, also juggling raising a child at home; it was time we introduced something new and refreshing. We felt it was time for a change and we needed a new revenue source that would not lead to burn-out. So we asked ourselves: "How can we generate extra revenue that will enable us to work shorter hours?" This led to us thinking about what actually troubles wedding couples the most. The answer: They don't even know how to get started with the planning of their weddings. Although there were (and still are) plenty of wedding blogs, magazines, and forums to choose from, couples still found it difficult because this led to information overflow. Readers can find all this information overwhelming and confusing. Because we had the necessary knowledge to plan a wedding and access to a vendor's network, we understood that not every couple would want to hire a wedding planner to take advantage of these resources. So, in order to create the extra revenue stream, we created our own wedding blog to build our email list by offering a step-by-step wedding planning guide. For those couples opting to go the D.I.Y. route, they could follow our guide book and ask us if they needed any assistance, giving us the opportunity to step in if required. As a result, we altered our business strategy from wedding planning to an online provider of wedding media that thrives on sponsorship and marketing.

Wedding couples come to us for help because they need "wedding inspirations"; they need ideas and the support of our network. When it comes to planning a wedding, there could be numerous ideas going through your mind and it is hard to decide and compromise, especially when it is your own wedding and there are emotional ties to each decision. After all, the bride and groom come from two different families, so it is not uncommon to have different expectations and requirements from the families. Our business is a challenge, but it is also a way to demonstrate our own capability in managing the clients' expectations, and to deliver using objectivity, but based on their values.

Do you have your own business idea? If so, congratulations! Go for it with passion and let it inspire you. If not, don't pressure on yourself. We are not all like Steve Jobs and Bill Gates; each of us has a unique set of skills and talents to offer and we are destined to discover them in time. Think of something that really tickles you and makes you smile, some place where your talents and skills meet; perhaps even giving you a competitive advantage. When you have the answer to this, you would have met with the inspiration necessary to follow your dream of starting a business. Any business you start will be challenging, but you will learn and it will all be worth it. Just keep inspired.

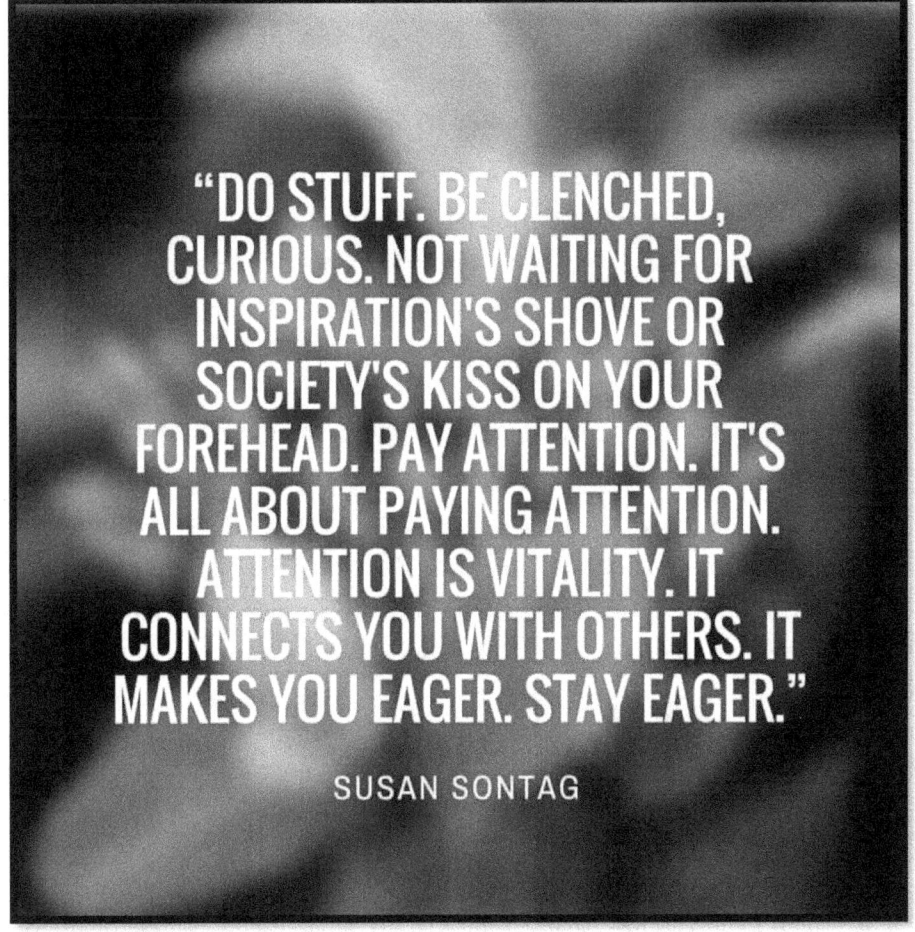

"J" - JOURNEY

I have always enjoyed hearing and reading about other people's success stories. Even when I was just an accounting professional working in corporates, I loved watching other departments doing their work and studying them intently. They opened me up to places I had yet to discover and showed me where I could fit myself in if I were to start my own business. Even today, I can spend hours at a time on Google searching for what I can learn from other entrepreneurs by zooming in and out of situations I face as a businesswoman from different angles. Learning is an important part of the journey, and knowing the facts by doing some research could save you from having to learn the lessons the hard way. That is part of being prepared.

When you let go of your corporate job, you are out of your comfort zone already. Sometimes you may find that you have great ideas but you don't receive positive feedback from the market or clients. You want to explore that further, but find out that the challenges facing you are not small at all. Businesses do have ups and downs and you find that things just don't turn out as expected most of the time. What do all these things tell you? You just have to understand that entrepreneurship is a journey, and it can be bumpy. It has its hills, mountains, and rivers to conquer. All you can do is put on your boots and trudge on. It is not uncommon to see start-up entrepreneurs work seven-day weeks trying to get through all these challenges. When I first started my company in 2008, working overnight at my business was not uncommon. But as time went by, I realized that status and results take time to build. You just cannot wait for perfection before you make the next move. You need to keep going with what you have;

gain the wisdom and experience; grow your network; and learn all the who's, what's, where's, when's, and why's.

Keep in mind that founding a startup is a long road; there will be lots of things to learn and to experience. You will need strength and courage to excel. Most importantly, you need to get started. It all starts with the first step and the longer you postpone taking that step, the harder it becomes to make it. This is why so many people who dream of being entrepreneurs never leave their jobs – they're too afraid to take the leap. You will be afraid, but do not let that fear overpower you.

Mike Balitsaris was left without shoes on a trip in Nicaragua. Mike's shoes were taken by the current while he was crossing a river during a rain storm, and as a result he had to put together a pair of sandals from an extra travel bag. The concept he designed turned into his very own footwear brand, the Waltzing Matilda, which offers different types of sandals. If Mike hadn't gone on the journey, letting it inspire his entrepreneurial spirit, and take him on a new journey in business and fashion; he may never have known what could have been.

There is never a dull day in the entrepreneur's life. Sure, there will be days that run smoothly, but they will not be dull if what you are doing is also what you are passionate about. You will see sides of people, places, and business that you may not have imagined before. In order to go on this journey, you need to expose yourself to it and get going. Some of us may have maps and plans for where we're going; but for most of us, we only know what the destination is and not necessarily how to get there – the map will be drawn as we go along, so bring an eraser so we can make corrections. We also don't know what to expect so come prepared with your gear, sense of exploration, and positive outlook.

Does it sound scary? Do you still want to come? Or would you rather stay at home, and work every day to build someone else's dream and not your own? If you're still curious, join me. We're in for an adventure of a lifetime (and it may just take that long)! Enjoy the journey of being your own boss. Find the time to relax, and reflect. Every phase that you go through is a part of your life and an experience that you should treasure.

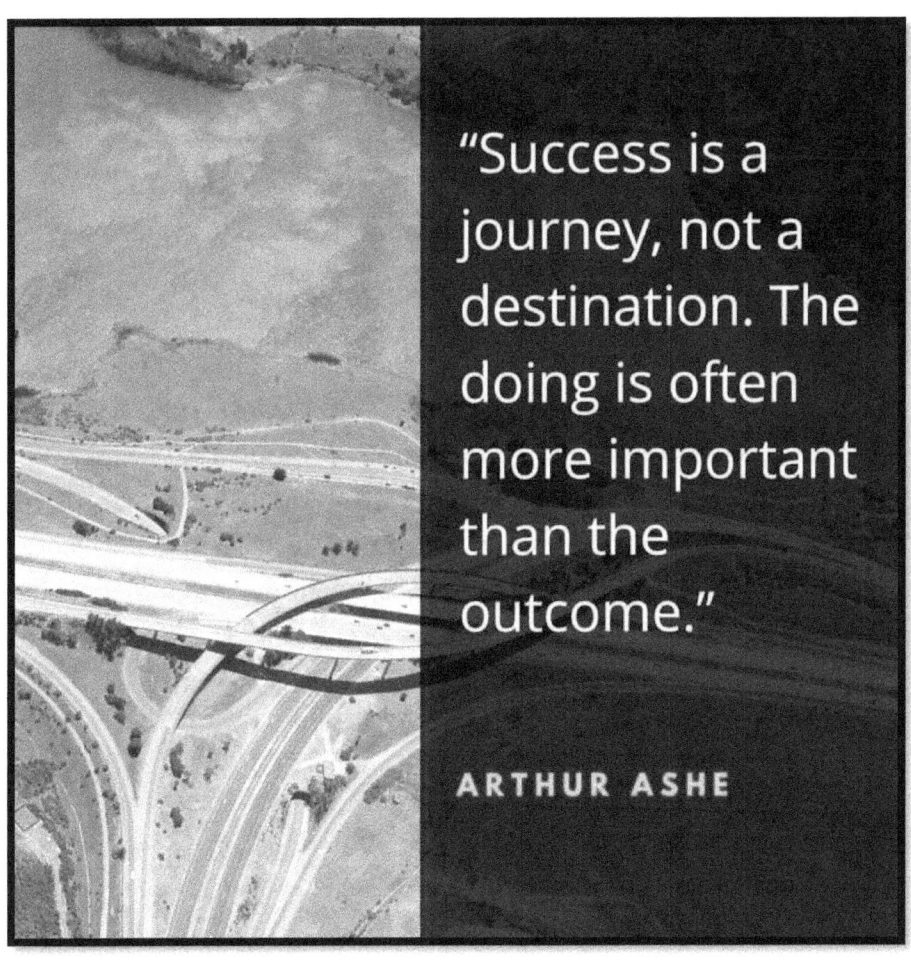

"K" - KNOWLEDGE

Why is "knowledge" important for an executive turned entrepreneur?

As entrepreneurs, we all go through our day-to-day lives aiming and yearning for success but a lot of things are easier said than done. We might be professional in what we have been doing in the corporate world, but we may be just like dummies in other areas. In the corporate world, we become very reliant on our personal assistants or secretaries. In some companies, when these people are absent, it is difficult for the business to carry on because often the personal assistant is the one who has a knowledge of everything that is going on, down to the last detail. On the other hand, during the start-up stage of your business, when it is your call for most of the business decisions, you may find that you don't have the right knowledge or skills to make things perfect. You will quickly pick up on your weaknesses when you have nobody else to rely on or to take the blame for you. On the up side, this will also help you hire the right people to fill in the gaps for you.

I would say that there are a lot of "soft" skills that are needed to keep things balance, or to take things forward, and keep going even in the face of hardship. For example, you may like to know the art of communication so that you have greater chances to close deals. When this is needed for your own business, you've got a much bigger incentive to keep learning. That is why I loved signing up with different mentors' websites as this is an efficient way to engage with like-minded people who can give you a push whenever necessary. It is not really necessary to pay and engage them as your mentor and often a regular newsletter will provide you with lots of know-hows on running a good business. These invaluable resources are just like a guide book that will point you to the right direction with insight and illumination.

Of course experience is crucial, but knowledge is essential. In this rapidly changing world, we all need to cultivate the habit of lifelong learning. Find ways to invest in yourself, and make time for learning no matter how hectic your schedule may be. Nowadays, some experts even go as far as saying that self-education can be more valuable than formal education. Although formal education provides direction and a solid foundation, you could potentially learn more from home by researching the things you really want to know. You will automatically retain more information if you are passionate about the subject, than when you are not. If you interests and business are directly linked to your learning, you will naturally make a mental note to remember the new information (although it is advisable to make a written note of it as well).

This is the information age, hence information moves at a rapid rate. A new piece of information can be released into the World Wide Web in a matter of seconds, changing the way that thousands, and possibly, millions of people do business. This is why it is important for you to stay in the loop. Frequently expand your knowledge in your areas of expertise and your business industry so that you are always aware of new opportunities or threats. This will help you offer better products and services as well as make informed business decisions.

Learning is amazing. It can transform you into a better, more successful person tomorrow than you are today. So let's keep learning to get to where we want to be faster and with more wisdom and knowledge behind us. Learning starts by trying to figure out where you are right now and what ignites your excitement. Once you've discovered that, you will want to learn more and more and that process will never end.

> "Formal education will make you a living; self-education will make you a fortune."
>
> — JIM ROHN

"L" - LEVERAGE

As professionals and top executives we have to understand that no matter how brilliant we are in our professional area, we are not superheroes and we cannot do everything by ourselves. So during the planning process for your own business, try to understand what skill sets you need, then build your team. You might think this would cost a lot of money. Not necessarily. There are a lot of people out there who would love to collaborate, so dare to share your ideas and exchange resources.

Let's recap what we learnt about levers in school. In physics terms, a lever is something (usually a long bar) which is pivoted on a fulcrum. The lever helps you move or open something. Now, imagine a business lever. The object you want to move is your goal, you want to take your dream from the ground up. You are the fulcrum and the lever is centered on you. The lever itself consists of the people and resources you have at your disposal. As a general rule, the longer the lever, the easier and faster it will be to achieve results.

Leverage comes when you are able to take advantage of other people's work, time, experience, ideas and money in order to progress in your business. Taking advantage of these things does not mean that the other parties are at a loss, but just the opposite. You and your team must be able to work on the same goal based on your vision and each person can contribute. Alone, you will never be able to do in two hours what two people could do in one hour. The more people you add to the mix, the greater your leverage when you can combine these skills and resources into achieving one common purpose.

Leverage is the key to speed in business. This is also why it is often quicker and easier for big businesses to make a change than it is for smaller ones. Yes, business decisions take longer in big businesses but when something needs to get done, they have the resources, workforce and experience to be able to do it quickly.

If you try to work alone, you will always be limited by your own skills and expertise. Successful entrepreneurs such as Henry Ford understood the power of leveraging off of those around you. Ford said: "I am not the smartest, but I surround myself with competent people." The founder of the auto manufacturer understood that he could not achieve his dream alone. He invested in other people and leveraged off of their talents. Today, Ford Motors is one of the largest global auto manufacturers as a result.

Business guru and motivational speaker Jim Rohn said, "You are the average of the five people you spend the most time with." Spending time with talented people increases your "average" and thus also your likelihood to succeed and succeed faster.

This is also how I started off my business Fiesta Wedding: I actually knew nothing about wedding planning, but one day I met an accountant friend who holds various wedding planning qualifications; he asked for my collaboration, and I said, "why not?" I could leverage his expertise and skills in doing the wedding coordination while I focused on sales and marketing to attract the brides. So we filled one another's gaps and shared the wedding profit. This was also a great opportunity to grow my jewelry business by setting up a bridal collection.

You can also leverage from your existing circumstances and resources. For example, the internet provides a tremendous amount of leverage. If you are online, you have access to thousands of people who could become potential partners, employees or clients. You have a huge leverage over somebody who may not have an internet connection and is thus limited to his/her physical reach and surroundings.

Another powerful leverage tool is having a mentor. Someone who has been where you are and tried to establish a business will know the pitfalls, struggles and obstacles. They will be able to guide and advise you so that you can avoid common mistakes and achieve success faster.

From the above, we can deduce that there are three forms of leverage – a team, network and a mentor. These three types of people provide different forms of leverage which can together fast track your path towards success. Have some names of people in mind already? Shoot them an email and leverage as much as you can. You'll be amazed at how many people will step forward to offer assistance; that's how you can grow your business.

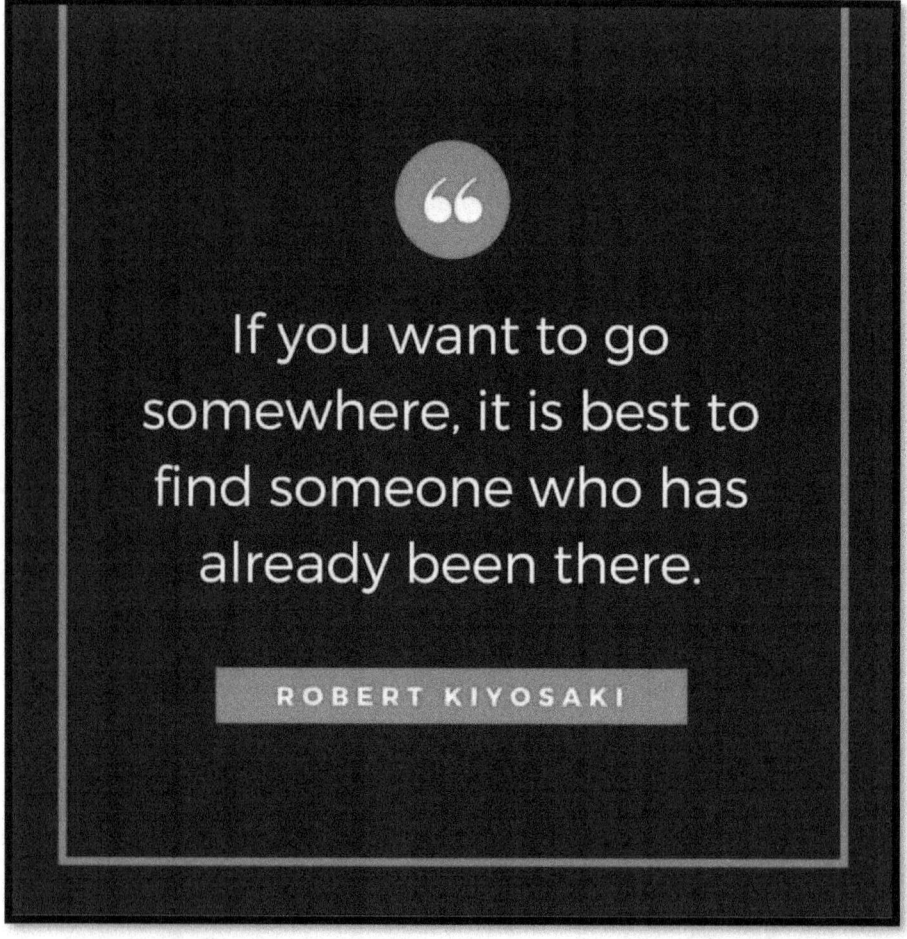

"M" - MARKETING

Over the past six years of running my own business, I spent most of my time building and maintaining my profile and reputation. A good profile is your most valuable asset, especially for home business owners. This is not something that you can buy, instead you earn it by honoring your promises. So if you already have a certain status in your profession, make use of your reputation and build the business. If you have yet to build a status, volunteer to help out in a network where you can find potential partners and customers. It is true that the more titles you gain, the higher your credibility will be in today's society.

So what's the best way to market your company? There are so many ways of doing this, but the best way to get the engine going is by doing things that you are familiar with. Social media may be one of them. In a time when Pope Benedict has also made use of Twitter to promote the church, you should seriously consider creating a professional presence on social media. Use Facebook, LinkedIn, Pinterest, Instagram, Tumblr, Google+ and other networks you can think of which may be relevant.

Without adequate marketing, no matter how good your product or service is, your business will fail. That is, if people don't know who and where you are, they cannot find you, and you cannot do business with them. We can use McDonald's to illustrate this. Ask yourself: Can I make a better burger than McDonald's? For most people, the answer is yes. The next question is: Then why does McDonald's sell more burgers than me? The answer: Marketing. McDonald's sells more burgers than anyone else because of an aggressive marketing plan. Everyone knows who they are, what they look like and where to find them. You may be thinking: But I don't have a marketing budget of millions of dollars like McDonald's. That may be true, but it is simpler today for small businesses to implement "big business" marketing strategies by harnessing the power of the internet.

Also remember that you cannot sell to everyone. Define your market early so that you don't end up trying to accommodate clients who don't fit into your business model later. This will save you time and money. There are more than enough fish in the sea, you need the ones that are actively interested in and looking for what you have to offer. When defining your market, draw up a profile for the perfect client. Include things like: budget (and income), social status, age, demographics, and interests.

Additionally, you can approach media or product reviewers and bloggers (who can reach out to your targeted audience) by inviting them to try out your product/service. What an independent party says is worth more than a thousand words that you can say about yourself. It only takes one person to make a difference so follow up is key. What do you want them to say? The product features and the associated benefits. Keep your advertising and sales messages consistent across different media. By doing this consistently and regularly, people will remember what you sell and the benefits of it.

Do you have a shoestring Budget? Just be creative as there are many people like you waiting to get to know each other so that you can barter, trade a banner, cross sell, or share the costs, etc. Dare to ask around.

When you post an advertisement, help readers to visualize what you are, what you do, and why they should come to you. We're living in a "time sensitive" generation, so when they come to you, make sure you respond quickly. Drop them a quick reply whenever you receive an enquiry, and get back as soon as you can. Show them that you care about them and make it as easy as you can for people to do business with you. This is how to build your good will and your business.

> As marketers, we should be changing the mantra from always be closing to always be caring.

JONATHAN LISTER

"N" - NETWORKING

If you come from a top executive background, you will understand how importantly networking can contribute to your business. Though such networking may not automatically bring business overnight, the way you follow up with the new connection, the relationship that you build along the way, and the synergies all count towards future business opportunities.

Networking increases leverage. The more people you can influence, the higher your success rate will be. This means that the more people you know, and more importantly the more people know you, will directly influence your results. For some startup entrepreneurs, networking can be a bit daunting but it needn't be. You don't have to speak to everyone at an event or make long speeches. All you need to do is be yourself and be approachable. I've noticed at many events that it is not always necessary to go out and talk to people; they will often come to you. After a few conversations and business card exchanges, you can leave each event richer in terms of your network. Of course, if you are more outgoing, the more you can contribute to network events, the better. Giving one speech to a roomful of people can create a lot of exposure.

In addition to physical one-on-one networking, you can take advantage of the most powerful and biggest network in the world today – the internet. The world wide web gives you access to networks where you can connect to millions of people and it takes a lot less time, effort and money than it would have a few years back. As a result, social media has become an essential part of doing business. Even if your business is not based on e-commerce, I still recommend you at least have a

Facebook, Twitter and LinkedIn page. Facebook itself is also a good example of the power of a network. The network has continued to grow since its inception and today has over 1.39 billion active users. As a result of the leverage of this network, the company sells advertising which brings in over USD $12.46 billion in annual revenue. Without the power and leverage of this large network of influence, Mark Zuckerburg would not be one of the wealthiest men in the world today.

When I jumped out from the finance area and started off my business, I still continued with my board position at the Association of Women Accountants. Not only did I wish to maintain my professional network there, but I thought to myself, "Many of these people could be potential clients as well." I even went further and joined some other associations so as to expand my reach. I also love to volunteer in running their events as this is a good way to demonstrate my ability and talents. This is especially true regarding the promotion of my wedding/event planning business. I once acted as the emcee at an annual dinner, and that not only gave me a lot compliments, but it also gave me new business. Volunteer work also creates a more complete profile.

Of course, you should choose your own relevant and quality networks to join. Take the time to surround yourself with quality people, who will unflinchingly give you their feedback. Remember that you are only as powerful as the size of your network and numbers are the name of the game (for both entrepreneurs and CPAs). Numbers reflect your bottom line, sales and potential. The more people you can contact, the better. Work hard to create, maintain and nurture your network. Also, remember that each member of your network is also the member of other networks. Therefore, nurturing your relationships with employees, partners and clients will go a long way. They will recommend you to their network and that may result in a sale and an increase in your network.

So go make a list of the people you already know. On average, each person has a network of about 250 people (your friends and contacts lists online should be a good indicator). After you have become aware of your existing network, work on growing your network and nurturing existing relationships. Go out for networking events and meet-ups. You could join trade associations or a Chamber of Commerce, or even meet new people on LinkedIn. Make friends by listening and offering good ideas. Be a part of the team!

> If you want to go fast, go alone.
> If you want to go far, go with others.
>
> — African proverb

"O" - OPPORTUNITIES

Entrepreneurs are essentially problem-solvers. When you see a problem, that's where an opportunity lies. This is how many entrepreneurs get inspired and find customers. Regardless what kind of business you are going to run, try to find and identify the problems that the clients or consumers are currently facing. When you find the things that trouble them the most and that you are eager to solve, that could be the business opportunity for you.

Having run my wedding planning business for around 3 years, I've done all kinds of sales proposals, marketing to brides and influencing them to book us for services. I asked myself, what else can I do to grow my revenue and diversify my income? How can I support those brides who do not plan to hire a planner, but want to plan their own weddings, with their own friends and family helping out with all the logistics? (This is where my aggressiveness tickles me again in thinking about how I can generate extra money from those who turned us down before.) My partner and I brainstormed this and I asked him, "What are the common problems you usually hear from your friends who are getting married?" (I was doing informal research.) And he simply replied, "They just don't know how to get started with their wedding planning." "What else?" I continued to ask. "They are afraid of approaching wedding planners as they think this may cost them a lot of money", he replied. Very true, most of the wedding websites in Hong Kong would just push all sorts of wedding suppliers' information to receive advertising revenue. I hadn't seen one which offered a simple yet informative planning guide, so we decided to do it ourselves. That's how I started my wedding media platform, Elegant-Wedding-Ideas.com which provides a Step-by-Step wedding planning guide and brings the unique elegant wedding ideas from the West to East. Not only does this help us gain the trust from those potential wedding clients, it also gives us extra advertising revenue by using a soft selling approach which promotes trustworthy suppliers. We differentiate ourselves from the regular local wedding websites by publishing our content in both English and Chinese, so as to attract both local and overseas brides who plan to get married in Hong Kong. This was our opportunity and now this new revenue stream accounts for approximately 12% of our annual revenue. It also brought us new wedding planning clients too. We also received a compliment from a bride who thanked us for the informative website which is written in both English and Chinese; she said she no longer required a translation for her fiancé who could only read English.

Another example of a monetized opportunity is the story of Tom Kulzer, the founder and CEO at AWeber, the email marketing software that I'm currently using. He was driven to build this multi-functional marketing tool as a result of a huge hurdle that he faced when following up with prospects. He found it difficult to contact many clients at the same time and keep them up to date with new developments and offers. So he developed AWeber from a one-man operation into a team of over 100, helping over 120,000 small businesses, non-profits and entrepreneurs around the world to reach more people with email newsletter campaigns.

Seeing the opportunities hidden beneath problems can sky-rocket your business. The key is to think positively and to always know that the opportunities are there. You can then choose which ones to act upon. Sometimes the seemingly small opportunities can have massive results. You need to plan to take advantage of the right opportunities and work to turn them into something which you can offer and sell to others. The work will pay off by creating something which will differentiate you from other product/service providers and will make a great impact with clients. The greatest opportunity is to serve your clients well. A happy client will thank you and boast about you to their network, creating free word-of-mouth advertising for your business, which will in turn result in more business opportunities. The cycle is never-ending so keep your eyes and ears open. Look around and find the opportunities. This will prepare you for the next big thing.

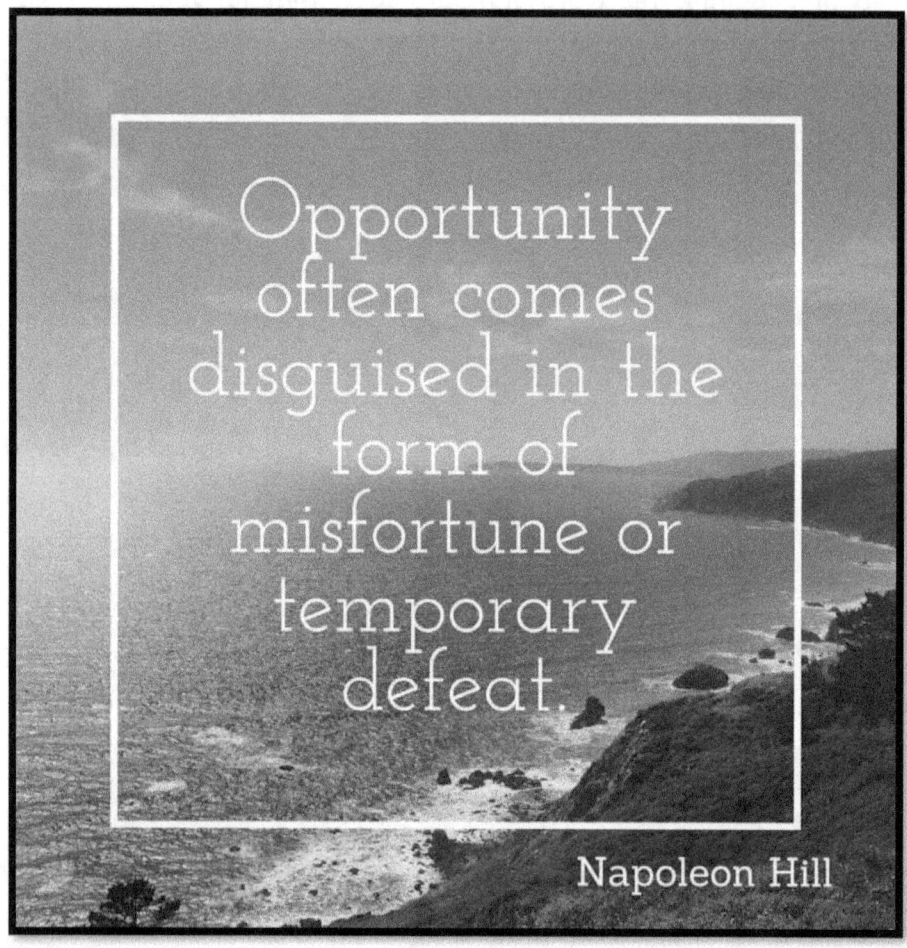

"P" - PASSION

Passion should be the driving force behind your endeavors. Without passion, you will eventually get bored and lose interest in what you are doing. That will result in you just using your business to make money and not to make a difference, and your clients will pick up on that. Anything which lacks passion will also not go very far, so rather than waste your time doing something which you think will make money, focus on something you love and are passionate about. Start with the passion and the money will follow.

If you listen to the stories of many successful entrepreneurs, they say that they had no idea that their businesses would be successful when they started. It often starts with a passion for something and wanting it to succeed. That passion and the action resulting from it attracts people to you because they want to be a part of it.

Elon Musk started programming when he was only 12 years old. At the time, he loved what he was doing, which later evolved to business services and products which have transformed online shopping, car manufacturing, and space exploration. Musk co-founded Paypal and then went on to found SpaceX and Tesla Motors. The former is revolutionizing space travel by reducing the costs of space exploration and transport with the aim of making it simpler and more accessible to travel to space and nearby planets, and the latter is a pioneer in clean energy luxury motor vehicles. Musk has a passion which drives his vision of the future. It is not only making him a lot of money, but also changing the world.

While working in corporate, you get used to 9 to 5, 40 hours a week, sometimes even longer. It can be tiring and draining. But when you run your own business, you will be so eager to work from the morning until late at night, or even overnight. You may wonder where this extra energy comes from. It's all driven by your passion. You would so much love to see the things that you are working on come to life, and you wish it to look the way that you want it to. And of course, "B.Y.O.B" – Be Your Own Boss. That is, you want to have your own business and take advantage of your new-found freedom and sense of control. Even though you may need to work for longer hours, you will still find it very enjoyable, and you will be happier than when you worked for a corporation. I have a very regular schedule, especially during the time when I need to take care of my son and work from home, for approximately 12 hours a day. But I don't feel tired as I'm so eager to turn my ideas into reality. I once had this slogan for my company: "Sparkle up Your Life!" It is this spark that kept me going and took my business off the ground.

So how do you keep this passion fire burning? Here's a few tips:

- Get together with like-minded people, who are positive thinkers.

- Read "success stories" from different business websites and magazines which you will be keep inspired.

- Get a mentor or join a mastermind group that you think could help you out. You need a constant push and lead especially during the kick start stage. I joined Ali Brown as she is very true to herself and she keeps you guided, directed and goal-oriented. I enjoy reading her work so much and many of my business associates agree. Best of all, it's affordable.

- Looking for something free? Join LinkedIn and participate in business groups that are relevant to your business. I have created a group called Achiever's Minds where I get together with professionals and executives from around the world and share business information and tips.

- Time flies quicker than before especially when you enjoy the things that you are doing. So make a monthly report of what you have accomplished. You will be amazed by the progress you have achieved, and will be eager to add new things to the report each following month.

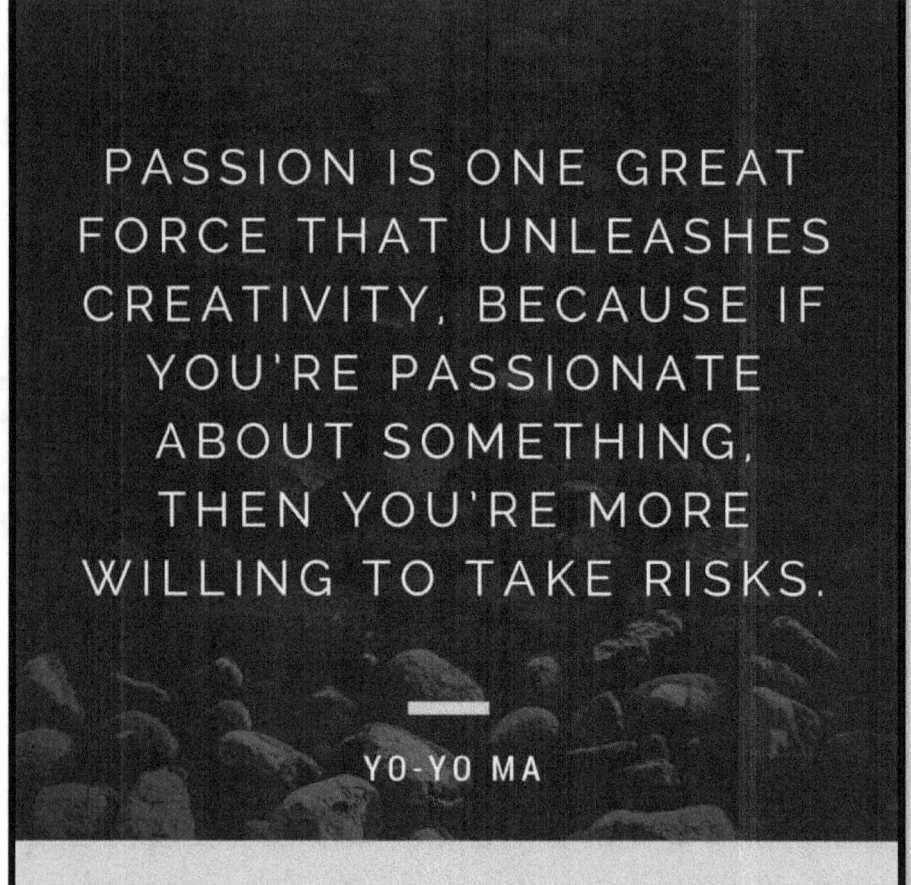

"Q" - QUALITY

The quality of your product or service is what will keep clients returning to you again and again as well as recommending your business to others. An easy online search will reveal the quality of a product as it has been described in reviews, and with this easy access to information, customer's expectations are getting higher and higher. So, in order to keep your business going, you need to invest serious time in quality, and uphold and increase that quality in order to develop a sound reputation.

I went to the supermarket the other day and I remembered to get a bottle of peppers. I found two bottles. The one was an unknown brand priced at USD $0.99 and the other was a well-known branded bottle priced at USD $8.00. They were almost the same size, and both contained peppers, so wouldn't it make sense to pick the cheaper bottle? However, the difference lies in the fact that the one bottle and its contents were manufactured in a Chinese factory, whereas the other came from Italy. Knowing this, I chose the bottle with the higher price tag for two reasons: China has been put in the spotlight for poor health regulations in food factories so I wanted to feel I opted for the healthier choice; and the Italian peppers were certified organic, giving me extra incentive in terms of making a healthier choice. I was willing to pay for better quality and because the manufacturer knows that their quality is better, they charge it at a premium. They have an established reputation and that serves as good leverage as well. This is why companies like to feature the year of their establishment with their branding, showing off their long histories. This shows a track record of delivery which is a very valuable asset to both your personal branding as well as for the company.

If you are in the luxury goods market in particular, it is all about quality. When buying a luxury item, you do not want to find out that the manufacturer tried to cut costs on materials and labor – you want them to invest in the best, as you are doing by buying their product. This is why people buy Bentleys, Ferraris, and Aston Martins – they expect the high price tag to come with a high quality standard as established by the relevant brand's reputation. An example of this has been the ongoing dispute between Apple and Android. For years Android developers have criticized Apple for limiting software development to the company. Apple responded by saying that their software is tailor-made to work directly with Apple iPhones and it is programmed to do this as best as possible. Sharing the software may compromise on the quality of the new upgrades. Whether you are an Apple fan or not, their products are arguably some of (if not the) best in the technology market, and the greatest contributing factor to this is a refusal to compromise on quality.

In terms of quality, there is also another aspect to look at and that is quality of life. This is measured by the quality of your interactions with your family and friends. One of the main reasons that I chose to start my own business was because I could work from home and as a result stay close to my child and family. Having the freedom to do this has changed my life and made it easier for me to make time for spending with loved ones. It does take a lot of discipline to stay focused when you have so many distractions, but keeping to your obligations pays off in leaps and bounds. We are a lucky generation that can do this! All you need to run your own business is a laptop and an internet connection, making it simpler than ever to improve your quality of life and reducing dead time spent in traffic and getting to and from work.

"R" - RISK MANAGEMENT

Entrepreneurs are risk takers. This is why many people don't dare to start their own businesses; they are too afraid of the risks involved. It may be safer to stay in the corporate world and earn a guaranteed monthly salary but that way you will never realize your true potential and what could happen if you go out on your own. Nothing was ever gained without someone taking some sort of risk. That is why when the stakes are high, the rewards (and possible losses) are also high. Taking a risk is like proof that you believe in your ideas, are passionate about them, and willing to see them through no matter what. You just need to be able to calculate risks and choose wisely regarding what types of risks you're willing to take. Although there is no fail-safe way to know if taking a risk is worth it, the more experience you gain, the better you'll be able to predict whether taking a risk is worth it or not. For example, you may be awarded with a year-long contract to produce certain goods/services. In order to meet the contract's demands, you may need to take out a loan for expenses. If you are successful, it will be no problem paying back the loan, but you still run the risk of taking out debt and having to pay back that debt even if things don't work out. You can evaluate that risk by weighing the amount of debt against the certainty and potential gain involved in the contract.

There are also risks which you cannot control. Do you still remember the recession happened in 2008? I started my company just a few months before it happened, and I still can't forget the many sleepless nights when the turmoil started to affect almost every country. People lost their jobs, and the stock market plumped. Customers cut their orders but bills kept coming. There were a lot of times that you just didn't know how long you could survive, no matter how passionate you were about the business. As a Certified Public Accountant, I was taught to be somewhat risk adverse so I was able to weigh the pros and cons in any decision. During that difficult period, I cut down all the unnecessary spending and looked for any potential business opportunities with the bare resources. As the old proverbs says, "cash is king" – I also disposed of some of the stocks as this global turmoil was really scary. I did learn a lesson after the global financial downturn. Owning a business is not always as glorious as you may think. There are always times when you must accept the reality that somethings are just out of your control. You have to be willing to deal with the possibility of failure. So no matter what you plan to do, give your best effort, hope for the best, but at the same time prepare for the worst too. As an entrepreneur, you will have to manage the money wisely and see every adversity as an opportunity.

What's more unfortunate is, in this competitive world, we are not only facing risks arising out of economic fluctuation, but also market conditions, new products, and even political environments. All of them can create different levels of risks to your business. In order to mitigate the risks, what you have to do is to constantly review the business environment, do your own research, and understand your strengths and weaknesses as well as that of your competitors.

Nina Simone is an icon in music, particularly Jazz. In the early 60s, a friend of hers arranged for her to get a job in Atlantic City, New Jersey. She travelled north from home and arrived only to discover that the club owner had expected a singer, and at the time she was just a pianist. He told her that if she wanted to keep the job, she'd have to sing and asked if she could sing. She'd never sung before but she knew one song so she risked embarrassing herself even further and being sent back home, but she took the opportunity and sang that song. The rest, as they say, is history.

Some risks are easier to evaluate than others. With some you may even need to risk it all, jump into the deep end and swim.

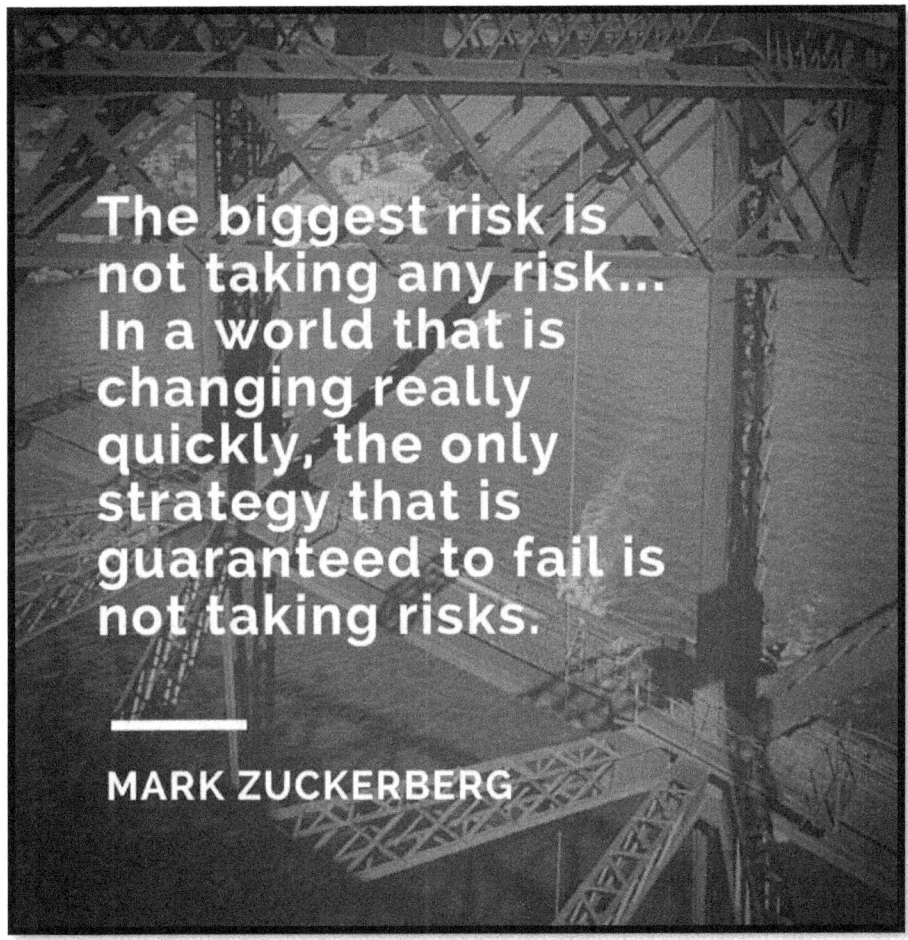

"S" - SELF-MOTIVATION

Being an entrepreneur sounds fantastic when you have passion, doesn't it? However, sometimes being an entrepreneur is not really as great as it may seem. When things do not go your way, without the self-motivation or perseverance, it will not be easy to go on. So you will have to create methods which will help you stay motivated. A successful business cannot be built overnight and there is no set rule or magic key for success, but one of the key traits for successful entrepreneurs is that they are always self-motivated. This means that they don't give up easily and are self-confident enough to always keep going. Business has its ups and downs, and you will have to treat failure as part of the journey. That way, you can program yourself to persist and move on whenever necessary.

Apple introduced the Macintosh computer to the market in 1984. Although it was the first mass market personal computer with a user interface and a mouse, it was expensive and failed to remain competitive in the market. A year later, Steve Jobs was fired from Apple and he would later refer to this as the best thing that could have happened to him. Jobs said at his commencement speech at Stanford University in 2005: "The heaviness of being successful was replaced by the lightness of being a beginner again, less sure about everything. It freed me to enter one of the most creative periods of my life." Jobs went on to found Next Computers and Pixar, before returning to Apple. His self-motivation and confidence kept him going when many others may have given up. If it wasn't for Jobs' perseverance, we may not have been introduced to 3D computerized animations, the iPhone, the iPad, and other devices which have revolutionized personal computing.

I remember when I started my jewelry business I was totally new in the field and did not have much knowledge. It was my passion for wanting to be involved with "pretty and glamourous glitters" that motivated me to take the GIA course and get the accredited qualification, thereby strengthening my confidence in dealing with customers. As a result, I've been able to keep going and carry on with the business, moving it to greater heights with every step.

How can you keep yourself motivated? Here's a few tips:

- Start first thing in the morning. Think of all the things you have to be grateful for, what you've achieved and your goals for the day, week, short term and long term. This way, you will automatically focus your attention on those things throughout the day.

- Regularly remind yourself of the things you've achieved and how much effort it took to achieve them. Think about personal accomplishments, professional achievements, awards you've received and credits you have gained. Personally, I remind myself of the hard work I invested in gaining my qualifications. I have my certified accountant qualification, the MBA, and the GIA, so I have to keep going and keep my professionalism.

- Set goals and stay aware of them. Make sure you know what your objectives are. What do you want to achieve by the end of the day? Where do you want to be in a week's, month's and a year's time? And where do you see yourself in five to ten years? By having a clear picture in your mind of where you want to be, you can stay focused on where you're going and the attainment of your ideals will keep you motivated. Define the short term goals that can help you achieve the long term goals. Revisit the strategy regularly to see how you can do better.

- Have a role model. Think of someone you admire and all the adversities they faced in order to achieve success. Ultimately, we are all capable of success so following a role model will teach you that you can also do it. Oprah Winfrey is my role model and I want to be as successful as she is. I keep following her network so as to gain insights on how to do things better.

- Be accountable. If nobody knows about your ambitions, then nobody can hold you to them. Confide in family, friends or colleagues who will support you in achieving what you want. You can also have a mentor who will guide you and invest in your progress.

Self-motivated individuals also tend to motivate those around them so you will have a positive impact on other people's lives. Never give up! Success is just ahead of you!

"T" - TRUSTWORTHINESS

I was once asked, "In running a business, do you think you will have to be sneaky in some ways in order to get your desired result or position?" That was a question from a lady in the top management of a multi-national company that invited me to give a talk to their ladies on International Women's Day. Honestly, I was shocked when she asked me this question, but I also replied immediately that it is not true. Instead, being sneaky will damage your reputation. You might be able to get a deal because you are sneaky enough to win it, but if you put yourself in other people's shoes, will they still continue to do business with you if they find they were actually cheating in some ways? Well, I would be angry and I would not bother to do more business with someone who cheated me.

I found a common problem amongst startup entrepreneurs. We all tend to over-commit to our clients or customers with a hope that they will give us the business. You might try your best to fulfill your commitments, but sometimes things do not turn out as you might have hoped. You may have overestimated our own capability, or relied too much on other partners or suppliers. At the end, when you fail to deliver what you committed to, this could cause a huge disappointment to the client and you will not able to gain their trust anymore. Adding salt to the wound, they may also give negative feedback as a result of the bad experience, which will harm your reputation with existing and potential clients. So instead of over-committing to something, what I rather do is set a reasonable expectation then over-deliver and exceed their expectations. Make sure that you only make business commitments that you know you can keep. Many entrepreneurs over-commit because they are desperate to have business constituents like and respect them, yet the quickest way to lose respect is to fail to keep commitments. Let your customers know you are trying to put them first and work in favor of them. Sometimes you cannot control other variables and you will fall short of what you promised to deliver. In such an event, own up as quickly as possible to the client so that they are aware of the situation. Trying to avert blame or hide from the situation may only make matters worse, and many clients will willingly empathize with you if they feel you are sincere in your efforts.

Honesty is the key to building your reputation. Never lie to your clients or business associates. Even "white lies" that may have been deemed necessary at the time could have huge negative repercussions. When clients feel that they can trust you, you'll find that they will be quicker to take your suggestions and make payments on time. Good clients will also offer bonuses and referrals if they are extremely happy with the products or services they receive. This is how you build your reputation, your testimonials, and attract the high end customers who are willing to pay for premium quality products/services.

Let's take Amazon as an example. The e-commerce giant has spent over twenty years building its reputation. When Amazon was first founded, people were still wary about ordering goods and making payments online. The company took steps to continually upgrade their system to make it more efficient, safe and user-friendly. Today millions of people shop on Amazon because it has a reputation for online security, reliability, unbiased product reviews, and an endless inventory of goods for sale. Price-sensitive consumers can also check the prices at Amazon before making any purchases, and for some people, shopping on Amazon has become simpler than going to physical retailers. In some places, Amazon even delivers right to the trunks of customers' cars. That's a lot of progress in two decades as a result of a glowing reputation which is portrayed by its expanding network of satisfied customers.

As with our personal lives, trust takes lots of time to build and can be shattered in an instant. This is why you need to carefully guard your businesses reputation. It is one of the best assets you have for growth, stability and ongoing success.

Trustworthiness

A leader's trustworthiness is the sum of his or her daily actions.

JENNIFER V. MILLER

"U" - UPCYCLE

Reusing information, ideas and resources wherever possible can stretch your business further and increase profits.

One of the things we did was upcycle our knowledge in order to create a new product to sell to customers we otherwise would not have been able to cater for. Wedding planning is a lucrative and rewarding career but also takes a lot of time and resources. After all, it is a "once-in-a-lifetime" event for every wedding couple and you want to do your best and fulfill their wishes. But at the same time, you need to take care of your own marketing, business development, public relations, etc. So I thought: "What would my life look like if, instead of being paid for my time to plan and orchestrate an event, I were able to turn my knowledge and experience, my tips (and tricks), everything I already know, into an automatic revenue generator?" The result was to upcycle my expertise to fulfill the various needs of wedding couples. Some marketing experts call this "information products" and I love this term. Information products are a way for you to sell your knowledge for the benefit of others. This book is an information product that you have purchased with the intent of gaining the knowledge I have shared to improve your own understanding about starting and running a business. I only had to write this book once. After it is marketed, it can be sold many times and will continue to earn royalties for as long as it is being bought by readers such as yourself. That is what is called "residual income", which is what one earns as a result of a product that is created once and can be sold many times over. The beauty of information products is that you can continue to earn royalties for a very long time without putting in too much extra effort. As time goes by, I may update this book and release new versions, but I will not have to rewrite it. The information serves as leverage so that I do not have to put in the same amount of time with every purchase. That is why I recommend information products. If you have helpful information you want to share, write it down. The quality of the information will help you gain a reputation as an expert and could be the starting point of a new business for you.

I feel honored that I was able to establish my status as an expert both as a wedding planner and a businesswoman by going into the industries and sharing relevant information. As a wedding planner, I was also able to increase understanding among clients and suppliers with the book. Clients are able to get an idea of what happens behind the scenes so that they know how much work and preparation goes into planning their big day. Suppliers are supported with the mentioning of their efforts and integrity of service, which creates incentive for them to continue to do business with us. I enjoy my existing lifestyle and on top of working one-on-one with my wedding clients, I am also contributing my expertise, which also gets get me paid. The extra source of income also frees up my time to do other things that matter like spending time with family.

Think about the different things that you can reuse or upcycle. Information is only one of them. Depending on your industry, there may be several ways in which you can upcycle resources. These resources could be tools that you can rent out when you are not using them or using your skills to consult for other companies when not working directly with your own clients.

So what are you waiting for? Upcycle now and get paid for your precious expertise and knowledge to generate a whole new income stream.

> **UPCYCLING ADDS VALUE BY TRANSFORMING OR REINVENTING AN OTHERWISE DISPOSABLE ITEM INTO SOMETHING OF HIGHER QUALITY.**
>
> ---
>
> WILLIAM MCDONOUGH

"V" - VISION

If you have worked for a big corporate, you know corporates like to have their vision statements up on the wall or at least published on their corporate websites. This serves as a reminder to all the people who work for and interact with the company about what it stands for. Some companies also hold annual functions to remind employees of the company vision, mission and objectives.

Vision is the first step in deciding to run your own business. It may just start out as a vision for a better lifestyle for yourself and evolve into something bigger as you progress. You need to know exactly where you want to go and what you want to achieve. Your vision is a picture of what the world will be like when your company is successful and it serves as a way to guide your steps towards realizing that vision.

If you have a passion for something, you usually have the associated vision even though you may not have it clearly written as the big corporates do. Personally, I don't have such a big vision like wanting to be the dominating business in a particular market or creating something that is life changing. All I want is to enjoy a better lifestyle with my own business, and if possible, do what I can to benefit the people around me. That works to drive me. You need to find what vision will drive you towards waking up every morning and putting 200% into your business. Businessmen like Donald Trump advise people to 'think big', but it is not necessarily about having huge goals as it is about making sure that your dream is big enough for you. We do not all want the same things out of life so make sure your vision aligns exactly with what you want. Forget about what others may have to say about it.

Larry Page and Sergey Brin founded Google in 1998 with the vision of creating a search engine which would make it simpler to find and navigate through webpages on the internet. After establishing itself as one of the biggest search engines on the web (today the biggest), Google started venturing into other products and services based on an expanding vision of technological innovation and automation. Today Google provides email services, blogging platforms, a social network, cloud storage, document sharing, eyewear, and driverless vehicles. These are only some of the services which have become a part of Google's vision that the founders could not have imagined when they first started out. With every new milestone the company reached, they were able to revisit their vision and create a new one. Google's vision evolved over time, and you may also hear celebrities and other notable personalities say that they had no idea that they would be so successful when they first started out.

So don't worry if you don't have a grand vision to start with. If you have a simple and easy to understand vision, write it down, tag it around your work place so that you can be reminded of what you are pursuing every day. Include it on your company's website and other promotional materials. Some vision statements even turn into catchy slogans. Make yours powerful enough to motivate you to pursue it and motivate others to want to be a part of it.

If you have a big dream, but it just doesn't turn out the way that you wanted it to, do not be stubborn. Change your focus and maybe there is another big market ahead. Also, don't give up on your vision. It takes many small steps to achieve something great and it would be a shame to turn around a few steps before you realize your vision simply because you didn't see that it was waiting right in front of you. Keep your eye on the prize and you will begin to be intuitive about your progress and success. We are not given talents and passions for nothing. Your own inner GPS system will tell you where you need to go and how close you are. You just need to switch it on, trust the directions and it will guide you to your destination or vision. Close your eyes and see your vision clearly, then start running towards it.

"W" - WORK FROM HOME

When I was still working in the corporate world, "work from home" was almost like a special privilege for executives like us. Sometimes it was even viewed as an unattainable ideal.

The advantage of being in the corporate world is that you feel secure. As long as you do your work and abide by the rules, you will get your salary at the end of the month. It's that simple. In exchange, you drive to and from work every day, often in traffic; and you're bound to the 9-to-5 lifestyle. You follow instructions from above and the system is structured so that with hard work, you can climb the corporate ladder in order to become a better paid employee. But, some of us yearn for more. We don't want to be employees our whole lives. Instead, we want to call the shots and be the creators of our own destinies.

On the other hand, when you start thinking about running your own business at home you might have doubts and wonder: "What will the family think of this arrangement? Will they worry about my earnings when I don't have a regular job?" These thoughts can be worrisome but the key is to get started and to keep working. The more successful you become, the more comfortable you will be about your decision.

STARTING YOUR OWN BUSINESS:

Most entrepreneurs start off by running their businesses from home. It saves them money, but it is not easy. There are distractions like television, kids, and perhaps worst of all, the great temptation to lie in bed all day.

A few tips to beat laziness and stay productive:

- Register a business address with a service center which is close to your home. They can support call handling, mail handling, and even offer meeting room facilities on a pay-as-you-go basis. Coming from a corporate background, you will want to have a formal office presence to maintain a professional business image.

- Set up a formal daily schedule. For example, get up at 7am, do some exercise, brew your own coffee and make your breakfast, then turn on the computer at 9am. Keep it as a regular as possible so that you keep the routine.

- Find out what motivates you. It is not easy being your own boss so you will need to refresh your motivation daily. Whether it's quotes, personal development books, audio courses or seminars; keep learning and sharing with others so that you remember that you are not on your own when it comes to building a business.

- Set goals. Know where you want you and your business to be in the short, medium and long term. Revisit these goals at least three times daily.

- Carve out a corner or a room just for work. Make it neat and tidy so that you are willing to stay there and work. If you need some fresh air, change to a different place for work, e.g. a café with a Wi-Fi service. This can give you inspiration too.

- Set up good communication systems for speaking to clients and colleagues. Skype is a good tool and it is free. Additionally, you can use your phone/email/text messages, etc. I also recommend setting a day or two apart every week to meet and discuss work with your colleagues and business partners at a certain time. This will make your work efficient, especially when everyone gets accustomed to this regular schedule. Everyone will know that their time at home is for work and not socializing.

- Set a daily time to switch off. This doesn't have to be every night, however if you're serious about working from home for the long haul, you have to make the lifestyle sustainable. That means you'll need time away from the computer and the stress of work.

- The most important part of running your own business is to stay focused. There are no presidents, supervisors or managers who will look over your shoulder to make sure that you are getting your work done. You have to manage everything yourself.

- Speak to family and people you live with so they understand and respect your work space and time. This is why it is also important to switch off. Let loved ones know that you will prioritize spending time with them for part of the day if they give you the needed space to build your business.

Many famous entrepreneurs work from home. Some telecommute so that wherever they go, their businesses go with them. Richard Branson, the founder of the Virgin Group in the UK, is often photographed working from his home on his privately-owned Necker Island in the Caribbean. Branson runs Virgin from the comfort of his holiday home with a mobile phone or laptop in hand. His business skills have made Virgin one of the largest corporations in the world and even some of his former employees such as AirAsia CEO Tony Fernandes have followed in Branson's footsteps and founded their own businesses.

Working from home can be the first step towards success in starting your own business. By keeping costs down, you can use the additional income to grow your business and accelerate your journey towards success.

It is all up to you. Your efforts can make or break the business but if you want to keep the freedom of working for yourself and create a potential future in which you can create a business system which can run itself and offer you more free time, you'll persist and keep working towards your goals.

Though working from home is not for everybody, once you get used to it, you will enjoy the freedom, the focus, and the extra family time so much. What you save is not just the office rental, but also the travelling time and cost, which can make you more productive in building your business than you are as an employee.

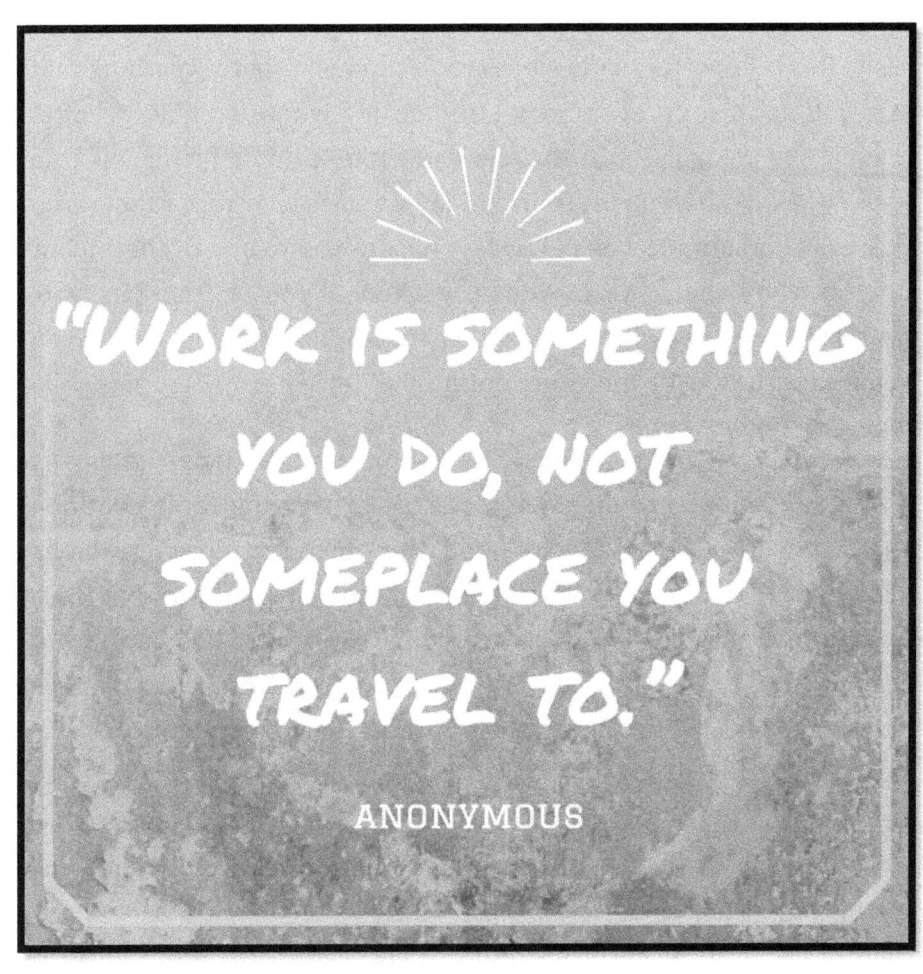

"X" - X-FACTOR

Nowadays "X-Factor" brings up images of a reality TV show. The original term represents the extra value or special something that someone might have to offer, which is what sets them apart from the rest. This is important in business too. You need that something that sets you apart from everybody else, making what you have to offer unique and valuable. But how do you acquire this X-factor? Is it in your DNA or can you create it? Many people want to be their own bosses (if you are reading my book, I'm sure you're one of them), but do you have what it takes you to get out of the nine-to-five work routine? Do you have the "X-Factor" that will push you to do it? In some cases it is just a matter of determination.

Take a look at various kinds of X-Factor competitions running in different countries; the leading contestants have the same common characteristic – determination (and the ability to sing very well). Whether the determination forms part of their characters or has been trained so that they are disciplined is not important. The point is that they possess a characteristic that is essential to success. We can even go deeper and look at the creator of the X-Factor franchise, Simon Cowell. He started off working menial jobs until his father managed to get him a job in the mail room at EMI Music Publishing. Following his success as a judge on the shows "Pop Idol" and "American Idol", Cowell started the X-Factor series, which has since branched out to many different countries and discovered many of today's popular music sensations. Cowell also started "Got Talent", where performers enter based on a talent of their choice. As a result, he has helped establish the careers of artists like Il Divo, One Direction and Susan Boyle. One can say that shows like the X-Factor were born because their creator possessed that "X-factor". Cowell kept going besides his past failures and kept working at his passion within the music industry. Today, the man who started out working in the mail room at EMI, now owns his own record label, his shows are household names, he has helped realize the dreams of many aspiring artists, and he has a net worth exceeding USD $470 million. That extra value or "X-factor" he had to offer has obviously paid off in leaps and bounds.

I was once told that investors look at the "X-Factor" rather than the business plan on its own. Do you have the "luck" or the "X-factor" that can lead you to successful entrepreneurship? Or do you think you can learn to build these strengths? Ask these questions in order to better understand your plan, but also keep in mind that the only true way you will realize the answers is by working at it. The more you dedicate to your business, the more your X-Factor will become apparent to you and those around you. And when your X-Factor shines, it will also become easier to attract other people who have that passion. For example, Cowell has attracted many business partners and talented people who possessed the X-Factor. You can attract the right partners and employees who are not just qualified to work with you but will add that distinctive touch that is unique to each of us.

Think about what sets you apart from everybody else? What is your "X-Factor"? Finding it may unlock the doors towards a path of future successes and there are no limits to the value of "x". As with algebra equations, find "x" and you will have the answer.

> **DID YOU KNOW**
>
> Believing in yourself is always the 'x-factor' in the equation of Achieving Greatness.
>
> ~ Timothy Pina

"Y" - YOUNG AT HEART

Age is just a number and it is often said that many people die at age 25 but are only buried at age 75. This is because they lose their sense of adventure and play, which can make life dull and boring. You may not still think of yourself as young, but you're on the right track if you are young at heart. Being young at heart means that you are still curious and eager to learn about things, and you are passionate about life, which you view as one great adventure.

If you started to read this book from Chapter A, then by this chapter you may have realized that being an entrepreneur is truly an adventure in life. There are lots of unknowns, yet there are also lots of possibilities. There are also many risks that require initiative to overcome. The challenges that come with running your own business that you are passionate about can be overcome with the type of zest for life that children naturally possess. If you feel you have lost it, it's up to you to work your way back to your roots and rediscover it by starting to take part in the things you enjoy. That way you will discover your passions, which will naturally trigger the feeling of beginning a wonderful journey, where you can learn along the way.

Some people also wonder when the best time is to start a business. Some say the sooner the better, but I recommend that you start later, after you have already built up your network and are comfortable with your experience and ability to produce wealth. However, there is no correct answer. This goes back to tapping into your natural instincts and making a decision that is best for you. If you feel unsure, you could test the waters by freelancing or starting a part-time business for extra money. Whichever way you start, remember to take your business seriously. Although you want to be young at heart, you need to still apply the wisdom that comes with adulthood – that is staying disciplined and focusing on your chosen path.

I still treasure my first few years working in a Big Four CPA company after my university graduation, where I was provided with the formal professional training and the experience of working in a big corporate environment. Having formal employment can help you grow traits like independence, professionalism, leadership, and charisma. Furthermore, a formal track record becomes important when you need to deal with other business men and women as you launch you own business. If you've got the ability and the drive, climbing the corporate ladder is the way to get started. That is the way I got started. You just need to realize when it is the right time to move on and pursue your dreams. I am still proud when I need to introduce my professional background and mention the places where I have worked before. In a job market that is becoming more and more qualification-centered, it will do you more good than harm to start out that way.

On the other hand, if you are already retired and thinking of owning a start-up, you are never too old to do it. Take a look at Colonel Sanders who started Kentucky Fried Chicken. Sanders was retired when he wanted to begin the restaurant franchise to sell his later-famous chicken recipe. He and his wife even lived in their car at a stage while he was approaching different restaurants. Do you know where he got his first investment? He took it from his Social Security benefits check when he was 62! A few years later the restaurants started approaching him, and Kentucky Fried Chicken (now KFC) became a major franchise and a multi-billion dollar corporation.

You are never too young or old for anything. Keep your young spirit alive and let your existing wisdom, experience, and network act as assets that you can invest in your business.

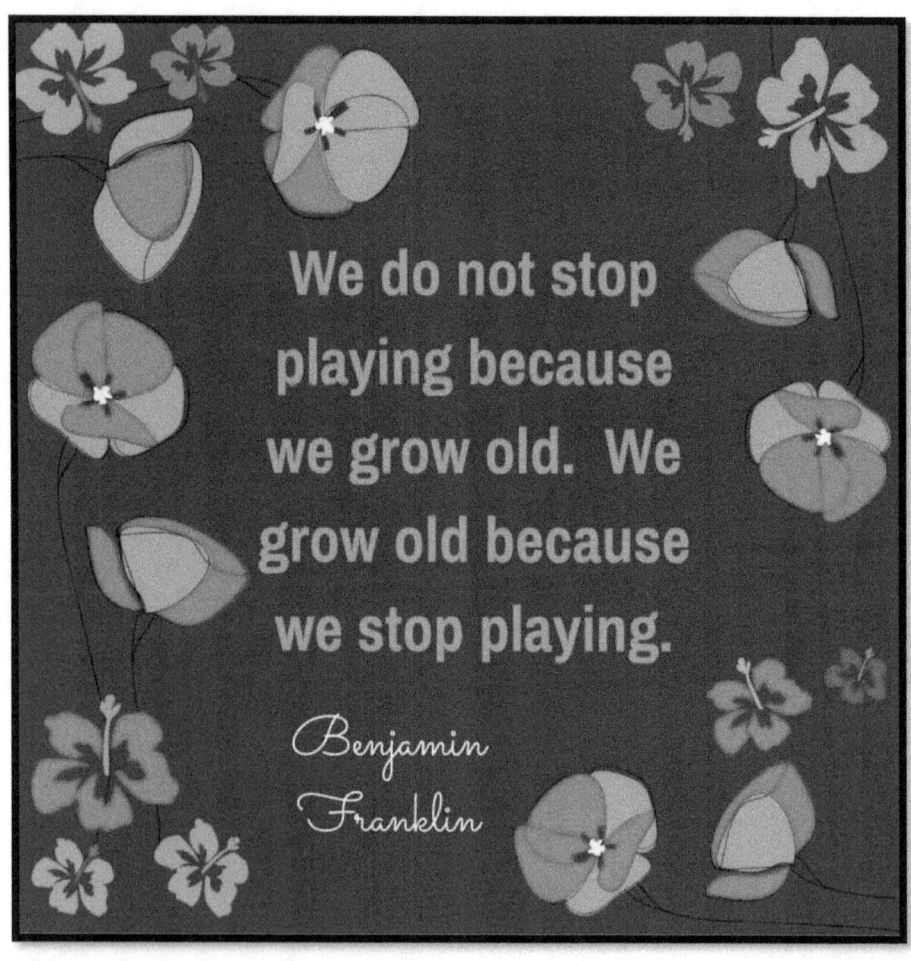

"Z" - ZERO TO ZILLION

Wow! So here we are at the last chapter. I wondered for some time what to write for "Z", and I decided to go for two extremes: zero and zillion. Don't get me wrong, I'm not saying being your own boss will either be all or nothing. Instead, bet small and think big!

Have you ever dreamt that being your own boss could make you a zillionaire? Look, we all want to make a good living, right? We are all gifted. Dream as big as you can. There are no limits. The possibilities of what you can do are literally limitless, even from a physical point of view. Every year we find out that outer space is bigger than previously thought and every year more and more money goes into circulation. There is more money to be earned today than there ever has been. Being a zillionaire may sound ridiculous but a decade back it sounded crazy to be a billionaire. Now there are trillions of dollars in circulation in single industries like healthcare, energy, and e-commerce. We've covered the last one quite a bit here – the internet is opening up more and more doors as you are reading this. So, take the leap. Yes, it will be hard work. And yes, it may take a while – maybe years, maybe decades. But yes, you can become a zillionaire!

Perhaps you're thinking: "I'll never need that much money." That may be true but the point is that a lot can be done with that money. Think of all the people you could help, think of all the causes you could contribute to. It is a fact that financial freedom is a huge factor in quality of life and the benefits could be exponential. It shouldn't be about getting rich, but usually when you find what you love and keep at it, the riches come to you. The world (on a smaller scale: your clients or customers) will reward you for the value you provide. Add more value and you will create more wealth for yourself. It is a numbers game. Large multi-national companies employ thousands of people and provide services to millions. That results in billions of dollars moving around providing families with food and their other necessities.

Sometimes it's difficult to measure the impact of one company until it starts making losses. Nokia used to be the leading smartphone manufacturer in the world. In 2008 sales started declining, resulting in a loss of 38 billion Euros until 2014. The job losses lead to a fall in Finland's GDP and it was estimated that the country would need 38 new start-ups with annual revenues of no less than 100 million Euros each in order to make up for the downfall. That's one large impact created by a company that was originally founded by two aspiring entrepreneurs, so never believe that you are too small to make a difference.

The case may be that you do not have much to begin with. Do not let that make you despondent. Many of today's millionaires were once homeless and desperate. They picked themselves out of dire situations to get to where they are. If they could do it, you can also do it, no matter what your existing circumstances. Start small and grow big. Start your business like you are running on zero (or very little) capital. That will also teach you to be mindful of expenses, and another trick to making more money is to save more money. It also allows you to become more creative in order to make things work on less.

Go on. You can do it. The first step to writing that first million-dollar check for yourself is to get going. Here's to your future zillions!

ZERO TO ZILLON

At least eighty percent of millionaires are self-made. That is, they started with nothing but ambition and energy, the same way most of us start.

Brian Tracy

YOUR JOURNEY

Chapters A to Z are definitely not an exhaustive list for executives or professionals who are thinking of letting go of corporate life to become their own bosses. However, I've selected the topics from A to Z as I believe that if you are willing to take action, these tips will help you get there faster and achieve greater success.

I also included my story to make my experiences relatable to some of you. I know I am blessed with an amazing life, which started with turning the passion button "ON", resulting in working on projects that I love, though they are not as glamorous as sometimes perceived. This is just like when we see other people's success, it was actually created by many years of struggle behind the scenes. My life is very different now. I spend less and less time working but enjoy more of my life while the business continues to grow.

Hopefully you'll take one or more of my ideas and run with it. I believe that the strategies and tools that I use can really help you too. I don't claim to know it all but as someone who is already crushing it, who has tested methods and failed only to get started again, I've had my share of experience. Now I am sharing my lessons with you so that you do not have to relearn them. This is not a "get rich quick" guide, but rather more of a "you can do it and here's how to get started" guide. You can do it without a technical background and not much to begin with, but the passion and will to get going. If I could do it, you can too. I was just a bored accountant who wanted to work on my own dreams. Now that's exactly what I'm doing. Here's to making your dreams a reality too. Good luck!

Hey!

 You can Dream.
You can set the Goal.
You can make it Happen.

Jane W.

ABOUT THE AUTHOR

Jane, who has always been described as a high achiever, is an ambitious, results-focused and resourceful person with a proven track record of surpassing financial and service objectives. Jane's extensive network and experience spans over 20 years in the areas of financial and business management, which has equipped her with the value of superb and exceptional interpersonal and people-management skills. This paved the way for starting her own jewelry business in 2008, named "Fiesta", which as the name tells, puts people in a happy mood with beautiful jewelry designed and produced in Europe. (www.fiesta-collection.com)

A strong work ethic and a broad range of experience allowed Jane to expand her business further into the event and wedding planning sector. Her capability in dealing with people at all levels and with different cultural backgrounds benefits her clients, who come from different nations, by providing a way to have a stress-free and enjoyable time at their major events. (www.fiesta-wedding.com and www.elegant-wedding-ideas.com)

With her extensive network, Jane has created a platform for executives and professionals to share daily resources for Management-Thought leadership. By learning from these high achievers' mindsets, you will realize that there is an order and a process of development in achieving your goal. If you are looking for ways to advance your business or let go and build your business, join Jane here on Achievers' Minds, where you'll find brilliant guides from around-the-world experts. Check it out here: www.achieversminds.com

Everyone needs a powerful network to receive recognition and to advance in career and business. Jane makes the connection here. Let's join her network and grow our businesses together.

Email: jane@achieversminds.com

www.ingramcontent.com/pod-product-compliance
Lightning Source LLC
Chambersburg PA
CBHW070258190526
45169CB00001B/456